The
BATHROOM
JOKE
ALMANAC

·

by

Jack Kreismer
and
Russ Edwards

RED-LETTER PRESS, INC.
Saddle River, New Jersey

THE BATHROOM JOKE ALMANAC
REVISED AND UPDATED 2018
COPYRIGHT ©2017 Red-Letter Press, Inc.
ISBN-13: 9781603871518
ISBN: 1603871519

Red-Letter Press, Inc.
P.O. Box 393
Saddle River, NJ 07458

www.Red-LetterPress.com

ACKNOWLEDGMENTS

BOOK DESIGN & TYPOGRAPHY:
Jeff Kreismer

•

COVER ART:
Design by Damonza

•

EDITORIAL:
Jeff Kreismer

•

RESEARCH & DEVELOPMENT:
Kobus Reyneke

The
BATHROOM
JOKE
ALMANAC

JANUARY

Today's Thought: "Now there are more overweight people in America than average-weight people. So overweight people are now average... which means, you have met your New Year's resolution." -Jay Leno

Observance/Event: January is National Prune Breakfast Month, National Oatmeal Month and National Fiber Focus Month. So since you're reading *The Bathroom Joke Almanac*, you're obviously right on top of things!

Graffiti: **Time wounds all heels!**

Joke: The girl said to her boyfriend, "Honey, I just had a dream that you gave me a diamond ring for the New Year. What does that mean?"
"You'll know tonight," he said.
That night he presented her a gift. She opened it to find a book titled *The Meaning of Dreams*.

JANUARY

Today's Thought: "The worst gift is a fruitcake. There is only one fruitcake in the entire world, and people keep sending it to each other." -Johnny Carson

Observance/Event: It's Fruitcake Toss Day- a pretty self-explanatory event if there ever was one.

Graffiti: **I used up all of my sick days, so I called in dead.**

Joke: Two army recruits are waiting in line to be vaccinated. One turns to his buddy and says, "What an outfit. We've only been in the Army for ten minutes and already we're presenting arms!"

If laughter is the best medicine, your face must be curing the world.

JANUARY

Today's Thought: "You can't have everything. Where would you put it?" -Steven Wright

Observance/Event: Someone thought to make this Drinking Straw Day. We'd say something about that being the last straw but that's almost as uncreative as the day itself.

Graffiti: **The Ten Commandments aren't multiple choice.**

Joke: A man was spread out over three seats, in the third row of a movie theater. The usher came by and said, "It is very inconsiderate of you to be taking up three seats. Where did you come from anyway?"
The man looked up at the usher and groaned, "The balcony."

JANUARY

Today's Thought: "Just when I found out the meaning of life, they changed it." -George Carlin

Observance/Event: It's Trivia Day, an annual observance to honor folks who know things like it's Independence Day in Burma, General Tom Thumb was born on this day in 1838 and the fact that today is Trivia Day.

Graffiti: **Square bathtubs don't have rings.**

Joke: Q: What do you call a cow with only two legs?
A: Lean Beef

My superpower is making people laugh, which would be great if I was trying to be funny.

JANUARY

Today's Thought: "The problem with the designated driver program, it's not a desirable job, but if you ever get sucked into doing it, have fun with it. At the end of the night, drop them off at the wrong house." -Jeff Foxworthy

Observance/Event: It's Twelfth Night, the end of Christmas and the time to take all those geese a-laying, turtledoves and pipers piping that your true love gave to you, back for an exchange.

Graffiti: **The days of the digital watch are numbered!**

Joke: Speaking of pipers piping, a plumber built up quite a business in Las Vegas specializing in casino bathrooms. His slogan was "A Flush Is Better Than A Full House."

JANUARY

Today's Thought: "A lot of people like snow. I find it unnecessary freezing of water." -Carl Reiner

Observance/Event: Two funny people were born on this day, *Saturday Night Live's* Kate McKinnon, in 1984, and Mr. Bean himself, Rowan Atkinson, in 1955.

Graffiti: **Miracle Drug- One that keeps you alive until you pay off the bill.**

Joke: Two caterpillars are talking to one another when all of a sudden, a butterfly goes by. The first caterpillar says to the second, "You'll never get me up in one of those things."

Letting the cat out of the bag is a whole lot easier than putting it back in.

JANUARY

Today's Thought: "It was so cold the politicians were walking around with their hands in their own pockets." -Bob Hope

Observance/Event: Millard Fillmore, the 13th president, was born on this day in 1800. His Know-Nothing Party didn't contribute much to history but Millard's birthday provides a great excuse to hold a party.

Graffiti: My Karma ran over your Dogma.

Joke: Q: Where was the crossword puzzle inventor buried?
A: 6' down, 3' across

JANUARY

Today's Thought: "Ever wonder if illiterate people get the full effect of alphabet soup?" -John Mendoza

Observance/Event: Speaking of soup, the legendary Soupy Sales was born on this day in 1930, in Wake Forest, North Carolina, because as Soupy put it, "I wanted to be near my mother."

Graffiti: Every town has gossip. If you don't hear it, you're it.

Joke: Two commuters struck up a conversation.
"I have four children," said one man proudly.
"Oh my, I wish I had four children," sighed the other.
"Don't you have any children?" asked his new friend sympathetically.
"Yeah, eight."

JANUARY

Today's Thought: "I'd like to come back as an oyster. Then I'd only have to be good September through April." -Gracie Allen

Observation/Event: They're hoisting a few fermented coconut milks on *Gilligan's Island* today, in memory of Bob Denver's birthday. Bob was born in New Rochelle, New York, in 1935.

Graffiti: **Seconds count...especially when dieting.**

Joke: Q: What do you get if you cross a lawyer with a snake?
A: A disgusted snake

JANUARY

Today's Thought: "I never got respect.
I remember when I was a kid and played hide and seek...
they wouldn't even look for me." -Rodney Dangerfield

Observance/Event: Celebrate Where's The Beef? Day. Wendy's cooked up this famous commercial on this day way back in 1984 and it really put them on a roll.

Graffiti: **He who hesitates loses his parking space!**

Joke: Two atoms are walking down the street and one says,
"I've been thinking. There's no doubt that I'm an ion."
"Are you sure?" the other atom asked incredulously.
"Yes, I'm positive."

Never hit a man with glasses. Hit him with a baseball bat.

JANUARY

Today's Thought: "Did you ever hear someone say this? 'It was more fun than a barrel full of monkeys.' Did you ever smell a barrel of monkeys?" -Steve Bluestein

Observance/Event: Got Milk? It's officially Milk Day today, which we're honoring with today's joke.

Graffiti: **Dogs hate shopping at flea markets.**

Joke: Q: What do you call a cow that can't give milk?
A: A milk dud

JANUARY

Today's Thought: "I just got back from a pleasure trip. I took my mother to the airport." -Henny Youngman

Observance/Event: Just a reminder that January is National Careers in Cosmetology Month. There's still time to enroll in a beauty school, although you might have to make up a couple of make-up tests. (Now it's officially Stupid Pun Day.)

Graffiti: **Stucco- what you get when you sit in gummo.**

Joke: Q: What's the difference between a mosquito and a fly?
A: You can't zip a mosquito.

If you're not supposed to eat at night, why is there a light bulb in the refrigerator?

JANUARY

Today's Thought: "Smoking kills. If you're killed, you've lost a very important part of your life." -Brooke Shields

Observance/Event: In 1910, Lee Deforest conducted the first radio broadcast to the public. Little did Deforest realize that all of those cat's whiskers, crystals and primitive vacuum tubes would lead to the invention of Howard Stern.

Graffiti: **A will is a dead giveaway.**

Joke: A talking dog walks into a bar and says, "How about a drink for the talking dog?"
The bartender answers, "OK, the toilet's right around the corner."

JANUARY

Today's Thought: "According to statistics, a man eats a prune every twenty seconds. I don't know who this fellow is, but I know where to find him." -Morey Amsterdam

Observance/Event: It was on this date in 1993 that funnyman David Letterman announced he was leaving NBC for CBS, where he would host *The Late Show* until 2015. As he said, "I cannot sing, dance or act; what else would I be but a talk show host?"

Graffiti: **They call it "revolving credit" because the interest makes your head spin!**

Joke: Q: What's the number one cause of death for hamsters?
A: Falling asleep at the wheel

Politicians and diapers have one thing in common. They should both be changed regularly, and for the same reason.

JANUARY

Today's Thought: "If you are going to tell people the truth, be funny or they'll kill you." -Billy Wilder

Observance/Event: Today is National Hat Day, a really serious observance, not to be confused with National Funny Hat Day which occurs on July 9th each year.

Graffiti: **Saints teach their dogs to heal.**

Joke: "Doctor, you've got to help me!" exclaimed the young man to the psychiatrist. "I keep imagining my body is covered in gold!" "Don't worry about a thing," answered the shrink. "It's very common. You have what we call a gilt complex."

JANUARY

Today's Thought: "Rarely is the questioned asked: Is our children learning?" -George W. Bush

Observance/Event: It's National Nothing Day, so if you have no plans, you're right in keeping with the spirit of the occasion.

Graffiti: **Old soap bars never die. They just bathe away.**

Joke: Q: Why did the racehorse sneak behind the tree?
A: To change his jockeys

What thinks the unthinkable? An itheburg.

JANUARY

Today's Thought: "Buy thermometers in the wintertime. They're much lower then." -Soupy Sales

Observance/Event: One of our favorite funny females, Betty White, was born today in 1928. So were two pretty funny guys- Jim Carrey, in 1962, and the late Andy Kaufman, in 1949.

Graffiti: **The Domino Theory: Eat enough pizza and you'll fall over.**

Joke: Little Johnny asked, "Grandpa, do you know how to make a sound like a frog?"
His grandfather replied, "Why, sure, Johnny. But why do you ask?"
Little Johnny answers, "Because Mommy says when you croak, we're going to Disney World."

JANUARY

Today's Thought: "What's the two things they tell you are healthiest to eat? Chicken and fish. You know what you should do? Combine them, eat a penguin." -Dave Attell

Observance/Event: Stand-up comedian Dave Attell was born on this day in 1965.

Graffiti: **How come noses run and feet smell?**

Joke: Hiring a new salesman, the boss warned him, "Now keep in mind that your salary is your business and no one else's."
"Certainly sir," replied the new employee, "and you don't have to worry. I'm as ashamed of it as you are."

Every so often, I like to go to the window, look up, and smile for a satellite picture.

JANUARY

Today's Thought: "Man is the only animal that blushes- or needs to." -Mark Twain

Observance/Event: One of the greatest of all Desilu Productions debuted today in 1953, Desi Arnaz Jr.

Graffiti: **Nuclear weapons are here to stay, but are we?**

Joke: Frick: I once knew a wealthy 80-year-old farmer who married a 20 year-old girl and couldn't keep his hands off of her.
Frack: Did she object?
Frick: No, so he fired every one of them!

JANUARY

Today's Thought: "Here's an interesting statistic. The world's population is growing by 170 people a minute, and still, the post office won't open another window." -Jay Leno

Observance/Event: It is the dawning of the month or so of Aquarius and famous comedic Aquarians born today. They include George Burns, 1896, and *Laugh-In's* Arte Johnson, who first got on the shtick in 1934.

Graffiti: **Always finish what you have sta........**

Joke: Q: Why are all dumb-blonde jokes one-liners?
A: So men can understand them

The Miss Universe pageant is fixed. All the winners are from Earth.

JANUARY

Today's Thought: "We got a name for sushi in Georgia- bait." -Blake Clark

Observance/Event: It's National Hugging Day so, as you read this, go ahead and squeeze the Charmin.

Graffiti: **People who live beyond their means should act their wage.**

Joke: "I bought one of those records that you play while you sleep and, in the morning, you know a new language."
"How'd it work?"
"Not so good. The record skipped and now I stutter in Spanish."

JANUARY

Today's Thought: "Some people are afraid of heights. I'm afraid of widths." -Steven Wright

Observance/Event: It's Answer Your Cat's Question Day. Some of our favorite answers are:
"Yes, dogs are incredibly gross."
"No, I don't know why they don't make Mouse McNuggets."
"Alright already!! I'll change the litter box!"

Graffiti: **Happy hour — because therapy is expensive.**

Joke: Q: Why did the pope cross the road?
A: He crosses everything.

There are two types of people in this world: those who crave closure.

JANUARY

Today's Thought: "I needed a password eight characters long so I picked Snow White and the Seven Dwarfs." -Nick Helm

Observance/Event: Believe it or not, it's Measure Your Feet Day, so get out that Brannock device and size up those footsies.

Graffiti: **Support bacteria! It's the only culture some people have.**

Joke: Three old geezers sitting on a porch watch a car speed by.
The first geezer says, "That Chevy was going awfully fast."
A week later the second geezer says, "That wasn't a Chevy, it was a Caddy."
A month later the third geezer says, "If you two are going to argue all the time, I'm leaving."

JANUARY

Today's Thought: "I gave my cat a bath the other day...he loved it. He sat there, he enjoyed it. It was fun for me. The fur would stick to my tongue but other than that..." -Steve Martin

Observance/Event: Russia's funniest export since they sold all of their nuclear waste to Eastern Europe as Pet Rockskis, Yakov Smirnoff was born in 1951.

Graffiti: **A thief is a man of convictions.**

Joke: Chester: A man knocked on my door today and asked for a small donation for the local swimming pool.
Lester: What did you give him?
Chester: A glass of water.

Never knock on Death's door. Ring the doorbell and run. He hates that.

JANUARY

Today's Thought: "All men make mistakes, but husbands just find out about them sooner." -Frank Coniff

Observance/Event: In 1915, Alexander Graham Bell placed the first transcontinental call to Thomas Watson in San Francisco. Later, just as Bell sat down to dinner, he got a call from a rival long distance company bugging him to switch.

Graffiti: **Two Err is Humin**

Joke: Q: What do you get when you cross a turkey with a centipede?
A: Drumsticks for everyone.

JANUARY

Today's Thought: "My grandmother started walking five miles a day when she was sixty. She's ninety-seven now, and we don't know where the hell she is." -Ellen DeGeneres

Observance/Event: Funny lady Ellen DeGeneres was born on this day in 1958. It's also Australia Day so have a G'day, Mate.

Graffiti: **Some "open minds" should be closed for repairs!**

Joke: A woman says to her physician, "Doctor you have to help me- I think I'm addicted to Twitter."
"Sorry," the doctor replies. "I don't follow you."

He who laughs last thinks slowest.

JANUARY

Today's Thought: "Have you ever noticed? Anyone going slower than you is an idiot and anyone going faster than you is a moron." -George Carlin

Observance/Event: Television was born in 1926 as inventor John Logie Baird first demonstrated the technology. The first television show? It was the face of an office boy seated in the downstairs laboratory. It was immediately followed by an infomercial about how to get rich quick in real estate.

Graffiti: **Parking is such a street sorrow!**

Joke: One penguin says to the other, "You look like you're wearing a tuxedo."
The other replies, "Who says I'm not?"

JANUARY

Today's Thought: "It's strange, isn't it? You stand in the middle of a library and go 'Aaaaagghhhh' and everyone just stares at you. But you do the same thing on an airplane, and everyone joins in." -Tommy Cooper

Observance/Event: Alphonso D'Abruzzo was born in 1936. He's better known as Hawkeye Pierce's alter-ego, Alan Alda.

Graffiti: **A clean tie will always attract the soup of the day.**

Joke: The after-dinner speaker droned on and on as more and more people got up and left. Finally the room was empty save for one other guy.
Frustrated, the blowhard stopped his speech and asked why the man hadn't left like everyone else. To which the guy replied, "Because I'm the next speaker."

JANUARY

Today's Thought: "It was always a good idea to keep a hip flask of Wild Turkey handy, as a stimulant, in case you see a snake, which you should also keep handy." -W.C. Fields

Observance/Event: Officially, W.C. Fields was born in Philadelphia on this day in 1880 although it may have been several years earlier. Old William Claude always liked to keep everyone guessing.

Graffiti: **A shotgun wedding is a case of wife or death.**

Joke: Teacher: If you stood facing north and your back was due south, what would be on your left hand?
Little Johnny: Fingers.

JANUARY

Today's Thought: "I really didn't say everything I said." -Yogi Berra

Observance/Event: The world got its first look at *Laugh-In's* Dick Martin's bippee on this day in 1932, and not in downtown Burbank either, but in Detroit, Michigan.

Graffiti: **Immorality is the morality of those who are having a better time than you are.**

Joke: A fellow is driving down a heavily flooded road after a torrential rainstorm when, all of the sudden, he sees a guy's head sticking out of a huge puddle. He stops and asks the guy if he needs a ride. The guy answers, "Nah, that's ok. I'm on my bike."

What is red and bad for your teeth? A brick.

JANUARY

Today's Thought: "I dream of a better tomorrow- a tomorrow where chickens can cross the road and not be questioned about their motives." -Roy Harry

Observance/Event: .yaD drawkcaB lanoitaN si yadoT

Graffiti: **Horse sense is what keeps horses from betting on people.**

Joke: Q: What's good for cold cuts?
A: Frozen Band-Aids

FEBRUARY

Today's Thought: "I moved to Florida because you don't have to shovel water." -James Randi

Observance/Event: Classic comedy troop members are part of today's birthday ensemble cast. Terry Jones of *Monty Python* was born in 1942, and Garret Morris of the original *Saturday Night Live* Not Ready For Prime Time Players made his first "live" appearance in New Orleans in 1937.

Graffiti: **Exercise daily. Eat wisely. Die anyway.**

Joke: Did you hear the one about the guy who wouldn't eat tongue sandwiches because they came out of an animal's mouth? He just had eggs for lunch.

I work to buy a car to go to work.

FEBRUARY

Today's Thought: "To you I'm an atheist. To God I'm the loyal opposition." -Woody Allen

Observance/Event: It's Groundhog Day. Ancient legend has it that if the groundhog emerges and doesn't see his shadow, then you will be blessed with an early spring. If, however, the groundhog sees his shadow, he's phoning it in from a beach in Aruba, so watch out!

Graffiti: **Fight air pollution- Inhale!**

Joke: A drunk staggers into a bar and yells, "Happy New Year!" The bartender says, "Hey, buddy, it's not January first. It's Groundhog Day."
The drunk slurs, "Oh no... My wife is gonna kill me!"

FEBRUARY

Today's Thought: "I bought a dog the other day. I named him Stay. It's fun to call him. 'Come here Stay!'" -Carrot Top

Observance/Event: It's National Carrot Cake Day, so everything's coming up carrot today.

Graffiti: **24 carrots are gold.**

Joke: Q: What did one snowman say to the other?
A: Does it smell like carrots to you?

Did you know that dolphins are so smart that within a few weeks of captivity they can train people to stand on the very edge of the pool and throw them fish?

FEBRUARY

Today's Thought: "I don't believe in astrology.
I think horoscopes are crap and all of us Libras feel the same way."
-Anonymous astronomy professor

Observance/Event: Two of the all-time biggest names in comedy share this birthday. David Brenner was born in 1945 and Dan Quayle in 1947.

Graffiti: **Robin Hood's house had a little John.**

Joke: Patient: Doc, my head hurts.
Doctor: I think I see the problem. You've got a piece of lettuce hanging out of your ear.
Patient: That's just the tip of the iceberg.

FEBRUARY

Today's Thought: "It's absolutely stupid that we live without an ozone layer. We have men, we've got rockets, we've got Saran Wrap – FIX IT!!!" -Lewis Black

Observance/Event: Today is Weatherman's Day, a time to remember that into each life, some rain must fall…especially on a weekend.

Graffiti: **A bachelor is a man who never makes the same mistake once.**

Joke: "Doc, I can't figure out what's wrong with me. I woke up today and called my wife Minnie. I put on some white gloves and on my way out the door started whistling, 'Hi ho, hi ho, it's off to work I go.' Then at the office I called my boss Grumpy and my secretary Cinderella."
"Not to worry- it's nothing major," says the doctor. "You're having Disney spells."

FEBRUARY

Today's Thought: "I asked God for a bike, but I know God doesn't work that way. So I stole a bike and asked for forgiveness." -Emo Philips

Observance/Event: Strange as it may seem, February not only is National Snack Food Month, National Cherry Month and Great American Pies Month. It's also National Children's Dental Health Month. Go figure.

Graffiti: **The meek may inherit the Earth, but it's the enterprising that'll be collecting the estate tax.**

Joke: Q: Why is Facebook a good site for loners?
A: Because it's the only place where they can talk to a wall and not be considered a loser.

FEBRUARY

Today's Thought: "A perfect vacation should be just long enough to make the boss miss you but not so long as to let him discover he can get along without you." -Sanford Mims

Observance/Event: Comedian Chris Rock was born on this day in 1965. It's also National Hangover Awareness Day- and since yesterday was Babe Ruth's birthday that makes this the morning after "Babe's Night Out," when some of the all-time greatest hangovers known to man have been survived.

Graffiti: **Bad dieters are usually poor losers!**

Joke: Did you hear about the cannibals who captured a group of politicians? They had to buy a crock pot to cook them.

The last thing I want to do is insult you. But it *is* on the list.

FEBRUARY

Today's Thought: "Economists report that a college education adds many thousands of dollars to a man's lifetime income, which he then spends sending his son to college." -Bill Vaughan

Observance/Event: Comedian Robert Klein was born on this date in 1942.

Graffiti: Have you hugged your porcupine today?

Joke: Then there was the guy that was so dumb, he lost his job as an inspector at the M&M factory. He kept rejecting all of the "Ws."

FEBRUARY

Today's Thought: "A good rule of thumb is if you've made it to thirty-five and your job still requires you to wear a name tag, you've probably made a serious vocational error." -Dennis Miller

Observance/Event: On this date in 1964, The Beatles made their first live American TV appearance on *The Ed Sullivan Show*, which leads us to this groaner- What did the boy octopus say to the girl octopus? ... "I want to hold your hand hand hand hand hand hand hand hand."

Graffiti: If flowers don't talk back to you, are they mums?

Joke: Q: What's the difference between the inside and the outside of a fireplug?
A: The liquid on the inside of a fireplug is H2O; on the outside of a fireplug it's K9P.

FEBRUARY

10

Today's Thought: "When I was a kid, I had two friends, and they were imaginary. They would only play with each other." -Rita Rudner

Observance/Event: The Great Schnozzola, Jimmy Durante, was born in New York City on this day in 1893.

Graffiti: **Unzipped mail is immoral.**

Joke: Knock Knock.
Who's There?
Control freak- Now you say, "Control freak who?"

FEBRUARY

11

Today's Thought: "I'm not a complete vegetarian. I only eat animals that have died in their sleep." -George Carlin

Observance/Event: On this day in 1960, Jack Paar walked off of the *Tonight Show* after an NBC censor had cut a mild "water closet" joke the night before.

Graffiti: **Experience is what allows you to recognize a mistake when you make it again.**

Joke: Q: What was the new home surgery kit called?
A: Suture self

The shinbone is a device for finding furniture in a dark room.

FEBRUARY

Today's Thought: "The problem with quotes on the Internet is you can never be certain if they're authentic."
-Abraham Lincoln

Observance/Event: Sharing a birthday with Abe Lincoln (1809) is funnyman Arsenio Hall, who was born on this date in 1955.

Graffiti: **Hypochondriacs can't leave well enough alone.**

Joke: Q: What kind of music do mummies like?
A: Rap

FEBRUARY

Today's Thought: "I hear YouTube, Twitter and Facebook are merging to form a super Social Media site-YouTwitFace." -Conan O'Brien

Observance/Event: It's Get a Different Name Day. If your parents hung a monstrous moniker on you, today's your chance to enjoy any name you please. Stefani Joanne Angelina Germanotta did and she became Lady Gaga.

Graffiti: **Alcohol is not the answer. It just makes you forget the question.**

Joke: A cop wrote out a speeding ticket. The recipient angrily began waving it in the air and said, "What am I supposed to do with this?"
"Keep it," said the cop. "When you collect three more, you get a bicycle."

FEBRUARY

14

Today's Thought: "Give me golf clubs, fresh air and a beautiful partner and you can keep my golf clubs and fresh air." -Jack Benny

Observance/Event: It's Valentine's Day and also the birthday of one of the all-time great laugh-makers, Jack Benny, born in 1894.

Graffiti: **Honesty is the best policy, but insanity is a better defense!**

Joke: "You don't want to go to court with me, Baxley. My lawyer's smart and he knows the law!"
"Well, then you really don't want to go to court with me, Grimsby. My lawyer's sexy and she knows the judge!"

FEBRUARY

15

Today's Thought: "When my son was born, I had this dream that he would grow up to be this Nobel Prize winner. But I also had another dream that he might grow up and have to say, 'Do you want fries with that?'" -Robin Williams

Observance/Event: Two late great funnymen were born on this day - Harvey Korman, in 1927, and Chris Farley, in 1964.

Graffiti: **Whoever named it "necking" was a poor judge of anatomy.**

Joke: Q: What do you call identical twins who wear a hairpiece?
A: Toupees in a pod

I'm having an introvert party and you're all not invited.

FEBRUARY

Today's Thought: "I can't stay- I'm leading a workshop on multiple personality disorders and it takes me forever to fill out these nametags." -Dr. Niles Crane (*Frasier*)

Observance/Event: It's National Do a Grouch a Favor Day, but, hey, if you're not up to the challenge, why not just sit back, relax and enjoy one of those *Grumpy Old Men* flicks.

Graffiti: **Ignorance is when you don't know something and someone finds it out.**

Joke: Q: What did the general do when he heard via Twitter that his troops were in trouble?
A: He retweeted.

FEBRUARY

Today's Thought: "It's amazing that the amount of news that happens in the world every day just exactly fits in the newspaper." -Jerry Seinfeld

Observance/Event: Git-r-done and wish Larry the Cable Guy a Happy Birthday today. The stand-up comedian was born Daniel Lawrence Whitney in 1963.

Graffiti: **An aquarium is a house of gill repute.**

Joke: Two birds are talking. One says to the other, "You look awful. Your feathers are frayed; your face looks like it was beaten to a pulp. What happened?"
"I got caught in a badminton game."

It's not a relationship until you argue about whose turn it is to apologize.

FEBRUARY

Today's Thought: "If most accidents happen within five miles of home, why don't we move ten miles away?" -Michael Davis

Observance/Event: Believe it or not, on this date in 1930, Elm Farm Ollie became the first cow to fly in an airplane. No, they didn't show any moo-vies on the flight.

Graffiti: **A polygon is a dead parrot.**

Joke: Did you hear about the unemployed school teacher? She has no class.

FEBRUARY

Today's Thought: "You know what I hate? Indian givers... No, I take that back." -Emo Phillips

Observance/Event: It's Temporary Insanity Day!! "S*&@^#$%"!!!!!!

Graffiti: **Surgeons make incision decisions.**

Joke: Army General: Do you have change for a dollar, soldier?
Private: I think so. Lemme see..
Army General: That's no way to talk to an officer. Let's try this again…Do you have change for a dollar?
Private: No, SIR!

A bartender is just a pharmacist with a limited inventory.

FEBRUARY

Today's Thought: "I got an 'A' in philosophy because I proved my professor didn't exist." -Judy Teneta

Observance/Event: It's the birthday of South African comedian and TV host Trevor Noah, born in 1984. And on this date in 1962, John Glenn was the first to orbit the earth, which reminds us: If athletes get athlete's foot, what do astronauts get? Missile-toe

Graffiti: **CIA agents are despised.**

Joke: I had a terrible dream last night. I dreamt I ate a giant marshmallow. When I woke up, my pillow was gone.

FEBRUARY

Today's Thought: "If the Lord had wanted people to fly, he would have made it simpler for people to get to the airport." -Milton Berle

Observance/Event: The woman who proclaimed that "any man who watches three consecutive football games should be declared legally dead", was born this date in 1927, humorist Erma Bombeck.

Graffiti: **What you seize is what you get!**

Joke: Patient: Doctor, I keep seeing double!
Doctor: Please, have a seat on the couch.
Patient: Which one?

My girlfriend told me to go out and get something that makes her look sexy- so I got drunk.

FEBRUARY

Today's Thought: "An earthquake is God grabbing the Earth and saying, 'cough'." -Richard Belzer

Observance/Event: It's George Washington's birthday…well, sort of. The date actually read the 11th when Washington was born, but due to a major adjustment to the Gregorian calendar, his birthday was bumped back to the 22nd! Back then, leap years must have been murder!

Graffiti: **Kamikazes do it once!**

Joke: Q: What's the difference between a trampoline and a lawyer?
A: You take your shoes off to jump on a trampoline.

FEBRUARY

Today's Thought: "After 12 years of therapy my psychiatrist said something that brought tears to my eyes. He said, 'No hablo ingles.'" -Ronnie Shakes

Observance/Event: On this day in 1874, Walter Winfield patented a game called "sphairistike", which became known as tennis. In recognition of the occasion, see today's joke.

Graffiti: **We are born naked, wet and hungry. Then things get worse.**

Joke: Q: How many tennis players does it take to change a light bulb?
A: "What do you mean it was out?! It was in!"

Despite the cost of living, have you noticed how popular it remains?

FEBRUARY

Today's Thought: "If a man is alone in a forest without a woman around, when he says something, is he still wrong?" -Bob Shulte, paraphrasing the age old "tree in a forest" question

Observance/Event: It's National Obnoxious Day. Be sure to pay tribute to those possessed of a putrid personality. After all, they make the rest of us look a lot better.

Graffiti: **A knob is a thing to adore.**

Joke: Q: What happened when the computer fell on the floor?
A: It slipped a disk.

FEBRUARY

Today's Thought: "The reason there are two senators for every state is so that one can be the designated driver." -Jay Leno

Observance/Event: It's Go to the Opera Day so call your local opera house and let them know you're "Carmen". This way, you'll end the day on a high note... Stand-up comic Carrot Top was also born on this day in 1965.

Graffiti: **Historians are a thing of the past.**

Joke: Q: What do you call twin police officers?
A: Copies

I drive way too fast to worry about cholesterol.

FEBRUARY

Today's Thought: "Anybody who goes to see a psychiatrist ought to have his head examined!" -Samuel Goldwyn

Observance/Event: "The Great One," Jackie Gleason, was born in 1916 and comic actor Tony Randall took his first bow in 1920.

Graffiti: **What this country needs is a good no scent cigar.**

Joke: A guy goes to a lawyer and asks how much he charges.
"Two hundred dollars for three questions."
"That's a lot of money, isn't it?"
"Yep, what's your final question?"

FEBRUARY

Today's Thought: "Why isn't 'phonetic' spelled the way it sounds?" -The Atomic Café

Observance/Event: Liz Taylor was born on this day in 1932. Her eight nuptials gave the world such jokes as "Liz Taylor's been married so many times she's got a wash 'n' wear wedding gown" and "What do they throw at Liz Taylor's wedding? Minute Rice."

Graffiti: **Don't put your foot down if you don't want it stepped on.**

Joke: The answer is despair... and the question?
What comes in handy when de tire goes flat?

I, for one, like Roman numerals.

FEBRUARY

28

Today's Thought: "I'm against picketing, but I don't know how to show it." -Mitch Hedberg

Observance/Event: Gilbert Gottfried was born on this day in 1955 and became a stand-up comic because, as he said, "I wanted to be a brain surgeon but I had a bad habit of dropping things."

Graffiti: **Man who puts face in punch bowl get punch in nose**

Joke: The roundest knight at King Arthur's round table was Sir Cumference. He acquired his size from too much pi.

FEBRUARY

29

Today's Thought: "A race track is where windows clean people." -Danny Thomas

Observance/Event: It's Bachelor's Day, a day fittingly celebrated only in leap years. After all, those guys are having a pretty good time of it the other 1,460 days too.

Graffiti: **Disintegrate Bigots!**

Joke: Q: What's LeBron James's favorite place to eat?
A: Dunkin' Donuts

I'm not saying that there's anything wrong with being left-handed. I'm just saying it's not right.

MARCH

Today's Thought: "If only I had a little humility, I'd be perfect." -Ted Turner

Observance/Event: It's National Pig Day, a day for those of the porcine persuasion to hog all the glory.

Graffiti: Pig farmers are disgruntled!

Joke: "Oh, Mrs. Owens," gushed the baby-sitter, visiting the maternity ward. "I can hardly believe it- triplets- how wonderful!" "Yes, it is, Sally," replied the proud mother. "Did you know that triplets only happen once in 4,657,842 times?" "4,657,842 times?" Sally gasped. "When did you ever find time to clean the house?"

MARCH

Today's Thought: "I'd rather go out with a perfect stranger than go on a blind date." -Patti Putnicki

Observance/Event: It's Peanut Butter Lovers Day, so whether you're dreamy for creamy or like to monkey with chunky, grind up those goobers and have the peanuttiest day that ever stuck to the roof of your mouth!

Graffiti: An editor makes a long story short.

Joke: Frick: Hey Frack, how'd you get the broken arm?
Frack: I told someone I was shy.
Frick: How did you get a broken arm by telling someone you're shy?
Frack: It was my bookie and I was shy about two grand.

MARCH

Today's Thought: "Military intelligence is a contradiction in terms." -Groucho Marx

Observance/Event: It's National Anthem Day, commemorating the anniversary of *The Star Spangled Banner* as our national anthem. The song narrowly beat out *America, the Beautiful, The Battle Hymn of the Republic* and *Isty-Bitsy Teeny-Weenie Yellow Polka-dot Bikini.*

Graffiti: **Is saltwater taffy seafood?**

Joke: Then there was the guy who had a short career in politics. In fact, the only time he ever ran for anything he was considered a write-off candidate.

MARCH

Today's Thought: "I've invented Twofacebook, the antisocial network. You start being friends with the entire world and defriend people one by one." -Andy Borowitz

Observance/Event: It's National Grammar Day. If you find any errors in this book, just know that it's our way of helping you to celebrate the occasion.

Graffiti: **H lp! S m b d st l ll th v w ls fr m th s gr ff t !**

Joke: A doctor called a patient and said, "Your check came back." The patient replied, "So did my bursitis."

As an outsider, what do you think of the human race?

MARCH

Today's Thought: "If we do not succeed, then we run the risk of failure." -Vice-President Dan Quayle

Observance/Event: March is National Noodle Month and National Sauce Month. The pasta-bilities are endless!

Graffiti: Care enough to be apathetic.

Joke: A guy tells his psychiatrist, "My wife thinks I have a problem because I like boxer shorts."
"That's no problem. I like boxer shorts myself."
"Really? With mustard or ketchup?"

MARCH

Today's Thought: "When I was born, the doctor took one look at my face, turned me over and said, 'Look, twins!'" -Rodney Dangerfield

Observance/Event: Humorist D.L. Hughley was born on this date in 1963.

Graffiti: Witches run spell-checkers.

Joke: At the Summer Olympic Games, a girl bumped into a guy carrying an eight-foot long stick. "Excuse me," said the girl, "but are you by any chance a pole vaulter?"
"Nein, I'm a German, but how did you know my name is Valter?"

Isn't it scary that doctors call what they do "practice"?

MARCH

Today's Thought: "I don't make jokes. I just watch the government and report the facts." -Will Rogers

Observance/Event: Funny lady Wanda Sykes was born on this day in 1964 in Portsmouth, Virginia, which is famous for, well, Wanda Sykes.

Graffiti: **If George Washington never told a lie, how'd he become president?**

Joke: Two fleas are standing on Fifth Avenue and 34th Street, planning to head up to New York's Central Park. One flea says to the other, "Shall we walk or take a dog?"

MARCH

Today's Thought: "You're not a kid anymore when you are obsessed with the thermostat." -Jeff Foxworthy

Observance/Event: This is National Procrastination Week. Or was that last week?

Graffiti: **In jail, you're here today and here tomorrow.**

Joke: Did you hear the one about the couple who wanted a civil wedding but decided on an open bar instead?

My wife is so negative. I remembered the car seat, the stroller, and the diaper bag. Despite that, all she can talk about is how I forgot the baby.

MARCH

Today's Thought: "The cost of living is going up and the chance of living's going down." -Flip Wilson

Observance/Event: Flip your calendar to March 9th and then flip your lid. It's Panic Day! (Although it would seem much more appropriate on April 15th.)

Graffiti: **Help wanted: Psychic (You know where to apply.)**

Joke: Q: What do you get if you cross a caterpillar with a parrot? A: A walkie-talkie

---

MARCH

Today's Thought: "Nothing in life is 'fun for the whole family'." -Jerry Seinfeld

Observance/Event: Alexander Graham Bell gave birth to Ma Bell today in 1876 with his invention of the telephone. In honor of the occasion, we bring you the following joke.

Graffiti: **Wrong numbers are never busy.**

Joke: Alexander Graham Bell worked day and night trying to perfect his new invention. Jubilant, he made his first call to his assistant, Watson. A voice answered, "I'm not in right now, but if you'll leave your name…"

There is a new trend in our office; everyone is putting names on their food. I saw it today, while I was eating a sandwich named Roger.

MARCH

Today's Thought: "That money talks, I'll not deny. I heard it once. It said, 'Goodbye'." -Richard Armour

Observance/Event: China's Ts'ai Lun invented paper on this day in 105 A.D. Bathroom readers everywhere owe him a debt of gratitude, in more ways than one.

Graffiti: Old accountants never die. They just lose their balance.

Joke: A couple of birds are sitting on a perch. One says to the other, "Do you smell fish?"

MARCH

Today's Thought: "Everyone should have kids. They are the greatest joy in the world. But they are also terrorists. You'll realize this as soon as they are born and they start using sleep deprivation to break you." -Ray Romano

Observance/Event: It's Girl Scout Day, which of course brings to mind cookies and that age-old question: Why do we cook bacon and bake cookies?

Graffiti: "Let me mix that salad." -Caesar

Joke: The wife of a prominent physician who was attending a convention in Las Vegas phoned the casino where she knew he'd be spending most of his time and asked to have him paged. "Sorry ma'am," she was told. "The house does not make doctor calls."

MARCH

Today's Thought: "If you live to the age of a hundred, you have made it, because very few people die past the age of a hundred." -George Burns

Observance/Event: It's "Uncle Sam's Day", marking the anniversary that everybody's richest uncle first made his appearance in the *New York Lantern* in 1852.

Graffiti: **Bad coffee is grounds for divorce!**

Joke: Q: How does Bugs Bunny stay in such great shape?
A: Hareobics

MARCH

Today's Thought: "The scientific theory I like best is that the rings of Saturn are composed entirely of lost airline luggage." -Mark Russell

Observance/Event: It's Moth er's Day and that's not a typo. Moth er's Day is a celebration mounted by museums who get their collections out of moth balls and proudly display them. It's the one time of year the spotlight is on the moths rather than the other way around...The spotlight's also on comedian Billy Crystal, who was born on this day in 1948.

Graffiti: **Old sailors never die; they just get a little dinghy.**

Joke: The answer is acoustic... and the question?
What do you use to shoot pool?

MARCH

15

Today's Thought: "Who invented the brush they leave next to the toilet? That thing hurts!" -Andy Andrews

Observance/Event: It's National Boss's Day Off, a time for bosses everywhere to sit back and take it easy. If, by chance, you feel you're too busy to just take the day off, remember what happened to Caesar when he showed up on the job on this date.

Graffiti: **Fortune tellers have a ball!**

Joke: Frick: Hey, how did you break your leg?
Frack: See those steps over there?
Frick: Yeah?
Frack: I didn't.

MARCH

16

Today's Thought: "My other brother-in-law died. He was a karate expert, then joined the army. The first time he saluted, he killed himself." -Henny Youngman

Observance/Event: On this date, in 1925, Joseph Levitch was born. You know him better as Jerry Lewis. Also born on this day in 1906 was the King of One-Liners, Henny Youngman.

Graffiti: **A toupee is a top secret.**

Joke: A Texas oilman was a constant bidder at an art auction and picked up three Van Goghs, four Picassos, a Rembrandt and a half dozen Monets for a cool $25 million.
On leaving, he was overheard to say to his wife, "Okay- so that takes care of the Christmas cards. Now all we need are the gifts."

MARCH

Today's Thought: My wife is an interior decorator. She wants to get rid of me because I clash with the drapes." -Morey Amsterdam

Observance/Event: The town that lays claim to the shortest Saint Patrick's Day parade is Maryville, Missouri. It's little more than 80 feet long and has been shrinking annually. Other towns must be green with envy!

Graffiti: **He who buys a mobile home doesn't get a lot.**

Joke: Q: What's green and stays out all night?
A: Paddy O' Furniture

MARCH

Today's Thought: "A lot of fellows nowadays have a B.A., M.D. or Ph.D. Unfortunately, they don't have a J.O.B." -"Fats" Domino

Observance/Event: Bathroom milestone- The Schick Company caused quite a buzz when they marketed the world's first electric razor on this day in 1931… Comedian Dane Cook was born on this day in 1972.

Graffiti: **The future isn't what it used to be!**

Joke: Q: If a cannibal ate his mother's sister, what would you call him?
A: An aunt-eater

You know you're ugly when it comes time for a group picture and they hand you the camera.

MARCH

19

Today's Thought: "My father was a successful businessman but he was ruined in the stock market crash.... A big stockbroker jumped out the window and fell on his pushcart." -Jackie Mason

Observance/Event: It's International Read to Me Day. You've got the material. Now go find someone to read to, uh, once you've completed whatever business is at hand.

Graffiti: **Parachutists jump for joy.**

Joke: A woman was driving her car and knitting at the same time. A motorcycle cop saw her, pulled alongside and said, "Pull over!" She rolled down the window and replied, "No! Mittens!"

MARCH

20

Today's Thought: "A cannibal is a guy who goes into a restaurant and orders the waiter." -Jack Benny

Observance/Event: Two of comedy's big guns got their shot at life on this day: Carl Reiner, in 1922, and Hal Linden, in 1931.

Graffiti: **Where there's a will, there's a lawyer.**

Joke: A lawyer, meeting with his client in prison, says, "I've got some good news and bad news."
The client says, "Gimme the bad news first."
"Your DNA matches the blood found on the victim as well as the murder weapon."
"What could the good news possibly be?" asks the client.
"Your cholesterol is down to 120."

You're the reason the gene pool needs a lifeguard.

MARCH

Today's Thought: "France is the only country where the money falls apart and you can't tear the toilet paper." -Billy Wilder

Observance/Event: It's the "Future Birthday of Captain James T. Kirk". Trekkies in Riverside, Iowa, believe that the real Captain Kirk will boldly go where some man has obviously gone before and be born in the year 2228. Don't worry, there's still plenty of time to pick out a card. Meanwhile, funny woman Rosie O'Donnell, born in 1962, is celebrating her birthday today.

Graffiti: Siamese twins make ends meet.

Joke: Q: What has a corncob pipe and a button nose and comes in the spring?
A: Frosty the Puddle

MARCH

Today's Thought: "When a man has to make a speech, the first thing he has to decide is what to say."-Gerald Ford

Observance/Event: It's National Goof-off Day, so just keep doing what you're doing. It's also the birthday of comic Keegan-Michael Key, born in 1971.

Graffiti: A butterfly is a worm that turned.

Joke: On Rodeo Drive in Beverly Hills, a sweet young thing walked into a boutique and called the clerk.
"Excuse me, but I'd like to try on the dress in the window."
"Sorry, miss," the clerk replied. "You'll have to use the dressing room like everyone else."

Any married man should forget his mistakes. There's no use in two people remembering the same thing.

MARCH

23

Today's Thought: "Nepotism isn't all that bad as long as you keep it in the family." -Winston Churchhill

Observance/Event: It's Near Miss Day. In 1989, an asteroid came within three hundred thousand miles of sending us the way of the dinosaurs. In space, that counts as a close shave.

Graffiti: **Why don't fish have to wait an hour after they eat to go swimming again?**

Joke: Then there was the guy who bought a defective boomerang. No matter how hard he tried, he couldn't return it.

MARCH

24

Today's Thought: "My father would say things that make no sense like, 'If I were the last person on Earth, some moron would make a left in front of me.'"-Louie Anderson

Observance/Event: Versatile comic Louie Anderson was born on this day in 1953.

Graffiti: **Organic farming is tilling it like it is.**

Joke: Two hillbillies are having a conversation. The first hillbilly says, "You know, it's a dog-eat-dog world out there."
The second one says, "Yeah, but it could be worse. It could be the other way around."

Doesn't expecting the unexpected make the unexpected become the expected?

MARCH

25

Today's Thought: "My ancestors wandered lost in the wilderness for 40 years because even in biblical times, men would not stop to ask for directions."-Elayne Boosler

Observance/Event: It's Pecan Day, commemorating the planting by George Washington of pecan trees at Mt. Vernon on this day in 1775. Not surprisingly, to this day whenever people hear the word "Washington," they think of a bunch of nuts.

Graffiti: **A timekeeper is a clock-eyed man.**

Joke: Q: Why do bees hum?
A: They can never remember the words.

MARCH

26

Today's Thought: "Big sisters are the crabgrass in the lawn of life." -Charles Schulz

Observance/Event: It's officially, or unofficially, Make up Your Own Holiday Day. Feel free to create your own special occasion. We sort of like *Bathroom Joke Almanac* Appreciation Day.

Graffiti: **Countries are making nuclear weapons like there's no tomorrow.**

Joke: A guy says to his buddy, "I'm thinking about buying a Labrador."
His pal warns, "That might not be such a good idea. Have you seen how many of their owners go blind?"

Two wrongs don't make a right; take your parents as an example.

MARCH

Today's Thought: "When cheese gets its picture taken, what does it say?" -George Carlin

Observance/Event: It's National Joe Day, a day for people with unusual first names to get to be like regular Joes, or Joannes as the case may be.

Graffiti: **Process servers put on the writs.**

Joke: Q: What's a Republican turkey?
A: One with two right wings

MARCH

Today's Thought: "Boy, those French: they have a different word for everything!" -Steve Martin

Observance/Event: Respect Your Cat Day marks the anniversary of King Richard II's 1384 edict condemning the consumption of cats. That is no doubt how he came to be known as "King Richard the Kitty-Hearted."

Graffiti: **A waist is a terrible thing to mind.**

Joke: A guy played cards with Siamese twins. When asked if he won, he replied, "Yes and no."

It is much easier to apologize than to ask for permission.

MARCH

Today's Thought: "The most important thing in acting is honesty. Once you've learned to fake that, you're in!" -Samuel Goldwyn

Observance/Event: It's Sing in the Shower Day, sponsored by _The Bathroom Joke Almanac_. Whether you're hardly able to croak a note or carry an aria, this is the day to croon your tune in the shower.

Graffiti: **The metric system doesn't measure up.**

Joke: "Doctor, we have an emergency! My baby just swallowed all of my tees!"
"I'll be there at once."
"What should I do until you get here, Doc?"
"Practice your putting."

MARCH

Today's Thought: "She got her good looks from her father. He's a plastic surgeon." -Groucho Marx

Observance/Event: It's "Doctor's Day"- and that reminds us of this burning question: Do doctors who treat people for amnesia make them pay in advance?

Graffiti: **Ballet keeps you on your toes.**

Joke: Q: What do you call a cow with no legs?
A: Ground beef

The grass may be greener on the other side, but at least you don't have to mow it.

MARCH

Today's Thought: "When you come to the fork in the road, take it." -Yogi Berra

Observance/Event: It's Eiffel Tower Day, honoring its completion in 1889, although to hear humorist Joey Adams tell it, the French landmark looks far from finished. "To me it looks like the Empire State Building after taxes."

Graffiti: **IRS: Income Removal Service**

Joke: "My, that's a beautiful diamond you have there," said one woman to the other.
"Yes, but it comes with a curse. This is the Klopman Diamond."
"Oh my!" said the wide-eyed admirer. "What's the curse?"
"Klopman."

APRIL

Today's Thought: "It's better to be looked over, than to be overlooked." -Mae West

Observance/Event: It's April Fool's Day so be on guard for those merry pranksters and their classic practical jokes like putting super glue on the toilet seat...Made you look- Gotcha!

Graffiti: **Curl up with a hairdresser.**

Joke: Wife: Honey, I've got some good news and bad news about the car.
Hubbie: Gimme the good news first.
Wife: The air bag works.

People who write "u" instead of "you"- What do you do with all the time you save?

APRIL

Today's Thought: "No matter how busy people are, they are never too busy to stop and talk about how busy they are." -Bob Phillips

Observance/Event: The first United States Mint was established in Philadelphia on this date in 1792. It's also the only mint that was ever shut down by a strike. The workers there wanted to make less money.

Graffiti: **Marshmallow peddling is a soft sell.**

Joke: The answer is: The Eiffel Tower. What's the question? What would the Empire State Building look like after taxes?

APRIL

Today's Thought: "A two-year-old is kind of like having a blender, but you don't have a top for it." -Jerry Seinfeld

Observance/Event: It's Don't Go To Work Unless It's Fun Day, actually part of a fortnight of fun and frolic including Discover Your Boss Has No Sense of Humor Day and Don't Bother Showing Up at The Unemployment Office, They're Never Going to Buy It Day… It's also Eddie Murphy Day. The comedian was born on this day in 1961.

Graffiti: **Good accountants keep you in the black and the IRS in the dark.**

Joke: And then there was the guy who got a job at the circus as a human cannonball. He was hired and fired the same night.

APRIL

Today's Thought: "Never learn to do anything: if you don't learn, you'll always find someone else to do it for you." -Mark Twain

Observance/Event: It's Dog Appreciation Month so pack up your pooper-scooper and give Fido a new leash on life as you take your best friend for a walk.

Graffiti: **Bad spellers of the world, untie!**

Joke: At Sunday school, the teacher was leading the class in a discussion of what Noah night have done to pass time on the ark.
"I think he went fishing," said the one little girl.
The little boy sitting alongside gave her a look and piped up, "What, with only two worms?"

APRIL

Today's Thought: "Adults are always asking little kids what they want to be when they grow up- 'cause they're looking for ideas." -Paula Poundstone

Observance/Event: It's Lady Luck Day so lay your cards on the table and be thankful when Dame Fortune smiles upon you.

Graffiti: **Whistler's mother was off her rocker.**

Joke: Q: How do you telephone a police dog?
A: Dial K911

There are few things I enjoy more than picking an argument with my girlfriend when she has the hiccups.

APRIL

Today's Thought: "If you don't want to work, you have to work to earn enough money so that you don't have to work." -Ogden Nash

Observance/Event: On this date, the North Pole was discovered in 1909 by Admiral Peary. Well, actually, it was discovered by a member of his expedition, Matthew Henson. Well actually, the North geographic Pole was discovered by one of the Henson's sled dogs who had waited a long time between trees.

Graffiti: **Down with everything that's up!**

Joke: Did you hear about the tiddlywink champ who had to retire? He sprained his wink finger.

APRIL

Today's Thought: "A vegetarian is a person who won't eat anything that can have children." -David Brenner

Observance/Event: It's No Housework Day. Skip the dishes, vacuuming, dusting and all that. Do nothing. As a matter of fact, we suggest you to start out the day by going back to bed.

Graffiti: **Soldiers do it fatigued.**

Joke: A woman was picking through the frozen turkeys at the supermarket, but couldn't find one large enough to suit her. She asked the stock boy, "Do these turkeys get any bigger?" The stock boy answered, "No ma'am, they're dead."

I need to start paying closer attention to stuff. I found out today my wife and I have separate names for the dog.

APRIL

Today's Thought: "There's a new iPhone app that lets you call your Facebook friends from your phone. Of course, I only got on Facebook so I wouldn't have to call these people." -Jimmy Fallon

Observance/Event: It's Zoo Lovers Day, which reminds us of the one about the cop who sees a guy walking a lion and says, "Hey, buddy. I thought I told you to take him to the zoo." The guy answers, "I did. Today I'm taking him to the movies."

Graffiti: **Happiness is having a scratch for every itch.**

Joke: Did you hear about the guy who drank 6 cups of coffee and 6 cups of decaf?
He stayed up half the night.

APRIL

Today's Thought: "If I had to describe myself in one word, it would be 'bad at following directions.'" -Matt Roller

Observance/Event: It's Longest Word Day, marketing the publication of a word of 207,000 letters in a scientific journal. Actually it was really a string of over 50,000 four-letter words spewed out by a scientist who had a Bunsen burner fall in his lap.

Graffiti: **Celibacy is not hereditary!**

Joke: Q: What do you call a dinosaur with an extensive vocabulary?
A: A thesaurus

My grandma told me her joints are getting weaker, so I told her to roll them tighter.

APRIL

Today's Thought: "Ever read the label on a deodorant can? 'Caution, content highly inflammable. May explode.' I don't want nothin' under my arm that's gonna explode!" -Richard Pryor

Observance/Event: The first professional golf tournament ever held in the United States was played at the Siwanoy Golf Course in Bronxville, New York in 1916. Accordingly, *The Bathroom Joke Almanac* pronounces this Golf Widow Day.

Graffiti: **Jack and Jill are over the hill.**

Joke: Q: What do clocks eat?
A: Mostly hours-d'oeuvres, in minute amounts, but they usually take seconds.

APRIL

Today's Thought: "'Buffet' is a French term. It means get up and get it yourself." -Greg Ray

Observance/Event: April is National Humor Month. Keep that in mind while filling out your tax forms.

Graffiti: **Life is like a shower- A wrong turn can leave you in hot water.**

Joke: A doctor says to his patient, "I have some bad news and some worse news. The bad news is that you have only 24 hours to live."
The patient say, "Oh no, what could be worse than that?"
"I forgot to tell you yesterday."

My therapist says I have a preoccupation with vengeance. We'll see about that.

APRIL

Today's Thought: "Insanity is hereditary; you can get it from your children." -Sam Levenson

Observance/Event: There's a smorgasbord of celebrations today: Grilled Cheese Sandwich Day, Be Kind To Your Lawyer Day (yeah, right), Library Workers Day, Licorice Day, Walk On Your Wild Side Day, and, oh yes, it's David Letterman's day. He was born on this day in 1947.

Graffiti: **Time flies like an arrow. Fruit flies like a banana.**

Joke: Q: What do you get if you cross an owl with a goat?
A: A hootenanny

APRIL

Today's Thought: "Until Eve arrived, this was a man's world." -Anonymous

Observance/Event: It's National Fresh Celery Month. It's crunch time so feel free to stalk your favorite vegetable.

Graffiti: **Get even. Live long enough to be a burden to your kids.**

Joke: Two old codgers were reminiscing. "My first girlfriend was named Mary Katherine Agnes Colleen Patricia Marion Margaret Kathleen O'Shaughnessey- I carved her name into a tree."
"What ever happened?" asked his friend.
"The tree fell on me."

If at first you don't succeed, destroy all evidence that you tried.

APRIL

Today's Thought: "Never eat more than you can lift." -Miss Piggy

Observance/Event: On this day in 1910, President Taft began the sports tradition of throwing out the first baseball of the season. Not that it has anything to do with the game, but we discovered that the 325-pound Taft once got stuck in the White House bathtub and had to be helped out by four men. Just thought you'd like to know.

Graffiti: **Parrots speak in polly-syllables.**

Joke: Q: What's the punishment for bigamy?
A: Two mothers-in-law

APRIL

Today's Thought: "There is one difference between a collector and a taxidermist- the taxidermist leaves the hide." -Mortimer Caplan

Observance/Event: The Titanic went down on this day in 1912 and since the federal income tax began in 1913, people have been getting a sinking feeling on this day ever since.

Graffiti: **The Ides of taxes are upon you.**

Joke: A beggar knocked on a rich man's door at 2 a.m.
"How dare you wake me up at this time!" yelled the rich guy.
The beggar replied, "Hey, I don't tell you how to run your business so don't tell me how to run mine!"

You're so old, when you were a kid rainbows were black and white.

APRIL

16

Today's Thought: "I thought I could do my own small part to save the planet by becoming a vegetarian. Actually, I did it not so much because I love animals but because I hate plants. I still like to hunt though. In fact, I've found that plants are a lot easier than animals to sneak up on." -A. Whitney Brown

Observance/Event: Stand-up comic Martin Lawrence was born on this day in 1965. And the long-running radio comedy *Fibber McGee and Molly* premiered in 1935.

Graffiti: **Enjoy daylight savings time- It'll probably be the only thing you save all year!**

Joke: Q: What do you call a monkey in a minefield?
A: A Baboom!

APRIL

17

Today's Thought: "I know that there are people in the world who do not love their fellow humans. I hate people like that." -Tom Lehrer

Observance/Event: On this day in 1629, the first horse arrived in America. Rumor has it that he walked into a tavern and the bartender said, "Hey." The horse said, "You read my mind, buddy."

Graffiti: **Love is blind but marriage is a real eye opener!**

Joke: Q: Where did they imprison the man who was convicted of assault and battery?
A: In a dry cell

I was born to be a pessimist. My blood type is B Negative.

APRIL

Today's Thought: "A new Facebook app is coming out that will remind users exactly what they were doing a year ago from that day. Nine times out of 10, the answer will be 'wasting your time on Facebook.'" -Conan O'Brien

Observance/Event: TV host Conan O'Brien was born on this date in 1963 while ventriloquist Jeff Dunham is a year older to the day.

Graffiti: **Clones are people two.**

Joke: Boxer: Doc, I can't get to sleep at night.
Doctor: Have you tried counting sheep?
Boxer: It doesn't work. Every time I get to nine I stand up.

APRIL

Today's Thought: "Vegetables are a must on a diet. I suggest carrot cake, zucchini bread, and pumpkin pie." -Garfield

Observance/Event: It's Ride A Bike Day, Garlic Day, and Hanging Out Day. Take your pick to celebrate (if it's garlic, you'll likely be hanging out by yourself).

Graffiti: **Old mufflers never die. They just get exhausted.**

Joke: A guy comes into a doctor's office with two bright red ears. "Doc, this is really dumb. I was at the ironing board and the phone rang and without thinking, I picked up the iron instead of the phone."
"Ouch! That's gotta hurt," said the doctor. "But what happened to the other ear?"
"Oh, that. They called back."

APRIL

20

Today's Thought: "When I was a boy, my mother wore a mood ring. Whenever she was in a good mood, it would turn blue. Whenever she was in a bad mood, it left a big red mark in the middle of my forehead." -Jeff Shaw

Observance/Event: It's National Recycling Month so remember, when you read an old joke, we're just doing our part.

Graffiti: **It's not the minutes spent at the table that expand your waistline...it's the seconds.**

Joke: The answer is Camelot ... and the question?
Where does a camel park?

APRIL

21

Today's Thought: "Well enough about me. Let's talk about you. What do you think of me?" -Bette Midler

Observance/Event: It's Holy Humor Month and here's our contribution: Two little brothers were troublemakers. One day a priest stopped one of them and asked, "Where is God?" The boy shrugged and the priest demanded, "I said, where is God?" The kid ran home, upstairs and into his brother's room. The brother said, "What's wrong?" The crying boy replied, "God is missing- and they think we did it!"

Graffiti: **The 11th Commandment: Thou shall not commit adulthood.**

Joke: Q: Why did the Amish couple divorce?
A: Because he was driving her buggy.

APRIL

Today's Thought: "A lot of couples shower together. It's supposed to be romantic and sensual. Truth? It's not at all as it's cracked up to be. Because one of you is not getter water; one of you, therefore, is not taking a shower." -Paul Reiser

Observance/Event: It's Be Careful What You Say Day. 'Nuff said.

Graffiti: Marriage- a knot tied by a minister, untied by a lawyer.

Joke: Q: How does a scared calf behave?
A: Cow-ardly

APRIL

Today's Thought: "Drinking make such fools of people and people are such fools to begin with, that it's compounding a felony." -Robert Benchley

Observance/Event: *The Bathroom Joke Almanac's* favorite form of social protest, the sit-in, was perfected on this date in 1968, as demonstrators closed down Columbia University.

Graffiti: Censors stick their "nos" into other people's business.

Joke: Receptionist: There's a man in the waiting room who thinks he's invisible.
Psychiatrist: Tell him I can't see him right now.

I've just written a song about tortillas; actually, it's more of a rap.

APRIL

Today's Thought: "The four stages of a man are infancy, childhood, adolescence and obsolescence." -Art Linkletter

Observance/Event: It's Cedric the Entertainer's birthday. The comedian/actor/TV host was born on this day in 1964. You can also celebrate Ambivalence Day...or not.

Graffiti: **No matter how much you hate reading prose- It could be verse.**

Joke: A woman called the town paper to place an obituary notice for her husband. She wanted it to read, "Farnsworth died."
The sales clerk said, "Would that be all? You could add three more words for the same price, lady."
The woman added, "Cadillac for sale."

APRIL

Today's Thought: "I used to play sports. Then I realized you can buy trophies. Now I'm good at everything." -Demetri Martin

Observance/Event: In England, April 25th is Cuckoo Day. In Washington D.C., every day is Cuckoo Day.

Graffiti: **Two wrongs might make a riot.**

Joke: A woman was doing some spring cleaning when she came across an old box with a shoe repair claim ticket in it. She brought it to the shoe repair shop and said to the owner, "Look at this. I brought my shoes here to be re-soled 10 years ago and forgot about it."
The owner replied, "They'll be ready next Tuesday."

APRIL

Today's Thought: "There's no better feeling in the world than a warm pizza box on your lap." -Kevin James

Observance/Event: It's the birthday of funnyman Kevin James, who was born on this date in 1965.

Graffiti: **If life is a waste of time and time is a waste of life, then let's all get wasted together and have the time of our lives.**

Joke: A doctor examines a woman, then goes into the waiting room and says to the husband, "I don't want to scare you, but I don't like the way your wife looks."
The husband says, "Me neither, but she's a wonderful cook and is good with the kids."

APRIL

Today's Thought: "It doesn't make sense. You're flying 500 mph, 30,000 feet in the air and the pilot tells you to feel free to roam around the plane. But when you're on the ground taxiing to the gate at one mph, he tells you to remain seated for your own safety."-Elayne Boosler

Observance/Event: The fourth Saturday in April brings the World Championship Cow Chip Throw to Beaver, Oklahoma. So if you're into bull slinging, limber up and go for the gold.

Graffiti: **Of all the things I've lost, I miss my mind the most.**

Joke: Did you hear the one about the glassblower who inhaled? He got a pane in the stomach.

APRIL

Today's Thought: "How come you never see a headline like 'Psychic Wins Lottery'?" -Jay Leno

Observance/Event: Comedian Jay Leno was born on this day in 1950. It's also Kiss-Your-Mate Day. Kiss your mate to show them how much you care. You'll probably get a kiss right back- unless you're in Australia, in which case kissing your "mate" will get you a punch in the kisser.

Graffiti: **Confucius say- Man with unchecked parachute will jump to conclusion.**

Joke: Did you hear about conjunctivitis.com?
It's a site for sore eyes.

APRIL

Today's Thought: "That silver medal at the Olympics, that's something, isn't it? You get gold, you've won. You get bronze, 'Well, at least I got something.' But silver is basically saying, 'Of everyone that lost, you were the best. No one lost ahead of you; you are the very best loser.'"
-Jerry Seinfeld

Observance/Event: Crack a smile as it's Moment of Laughter Day. It's also the birthday of someone who's given us many of those moments, Jerry Seinfeld, who was born in 1954.

Graffiti: **Anarchy rules!**

Joke: Q: What do you get when you cross a teacher with a vampire?
A: Lots of blood tests.

APRIL

Today's Thought: "Cars will soon have the Internet on the dashboard. I worry that this will distract me from my texting." -Andy Borowitz

Observance/Event: It's National Honesty Day. Really! Would we lie to you?

Graffiti: **If at first you don't succeed- cheat!**

Joke: A man goes to a psychiatrist office, takes out a pouch of pipe tobacco and sticks it in his ear. Seeing this, the psychiatrist says, "It seems you've come to the right place. How may I help you?" The guy replies, "You can give me a light."

MAY

Today's Thought: "Men who consistently leave the toilet seat up secretly want women to get up to go the bathroom in the middle of the night and fall in." -Rita Rudner

Observance/Event: May is Correct Posture Month and *The Bathroom Joke Almanac* is just what the doctor ordered for a slumping slouch. All month long, whenever you're sitting in the bathroom, close the book and place it on your head.

Graffiti: **Here I sit, my dignity tarnished, The toilet seat was freshly varnished.**

Joke: Did you hear the one about the book on levitation? You just can't put it down.

I broke my finger last week. On the other hand, I'm okay.

MAY

Today's Thought: "There's a pizza place near where I live that sells only slices. In the back, you can see a guy tossing a triangle in the air." -Steven Wright

Observance/Event: You'll find a lot of crabs at the Jersey Shore, but the only one who has his own day is Martin Z. Mollusk, Ocean City's official hermit crab. If he sees his shadow on the first Thursday in May, summer comes a week early and that means some tourists will step on him a week sooner.

Graffiti: **If love is blind, why is lingerie so popular?**

Joke: "Waiter, there is a fly in my soup."
"Could be. The chef used to be a tailor."

MAY

Today's Thought: "My fake plants died because I did not pretend to water them." -Mitch Hedberg

Observance/Event: It's Lumpy Rug Day. Not only is this event celebrated coast-to-coast, it's observed wall-to-wall.

Graffiti: **What do you say when an atheist sneezes?**

Joke: A woman calls in sick to work. Her boss asks, "What's wrong?"
She says, "I have occupational glaucoma."
"What's that?" he asks.
"I just can't see coming into work today."

Take my advice. I'm not using it.

MAY

Today's Thought: "Despite constant warning, you never met anybody who has had their arm broken by a swan." -Peter Kay

Observance/Event: It's Naked Day – okay if you're in the bathroom, but we're not responsible otherwise.

Graffiti: **My mother was the travel agent for guilt trips.**

Joke: Patient: Doc, everybody takes advantage of me!
Psychiatrist: That's quite normal.
Patient: Really? That's great! How much do I owe you?
Psychiatrist: How much have you got?

MAY

Today's Thought: "Latinos outnumber black people now. I'm not too happy about it. It's only a matter of time before we lose our month. Soon as they figure it out they're gonna have Latino History Month, and all we'll have left is Cinco de Negro." -Alonzo Bodden

Observance/Event: It's Cinco de Mayo! On another celebratory note, Password Day is celebrated the first Thursday of May. In honor of the occasion, here's some sound advice not to use. Change all your passwords to "incorrect". That way, whenever you forget, you'll be told, "Your password is incorrect."

Graffiti: **You can lead a man to water but you can't make him put the seat back down.**

Joke: And then there was the would-be entrepreneur who was duped into buying hundreds of cases of Cheerios. He was told that they were bagel seeds.

MAY

Today's Thought: "I'm on that diet where you eat vegetables and drink wine. That's a good diet. I lost ten pounds and my driver's license." -Larry The Cable Guy

Observance/Event: It's International No Diet Day and - how convenient - it's also National Hoagie Day.

Graffiti: **When you jump to conclusions, there is never a safety net.**

Joke: There was a two-car accident. The driver of the car that was rear-ended was a dwarf. He got out of his car, looked at the damage and said, "I'm not happy."
The other driver said, "Well, which one are you then?"

MAY

Today's Thought: "If you don't know where you're going, you could wind up someplace else." -Yogi Berra

Observance/Event: May is Fungal Infection Awareness Month. 'Nuff said.

Graffiti: **A school is a mental institution.**

Joke: The expectant father had a furrowed brow.
"What's the matter?" asked the other man in the maternity ward waiting room.
"My wife read *Tale of Two Cities* and had twins. The next year she read *The Three Musketeers* and had triplets," replied the nervous father.
"So?"
"She just finished *Birth of a Nation*!"

MAY

Today's Thought: "A computer once beat me at chess, but it was no match for me at kickboxing." -Emo Philips

Observance/Event: The Merchant of Venom, Don Rickles, was born on this day in 1926. It's also No Socks Day, a casual dress day for your feet. Every May 8th, people across the country choose to kick up their heels and step out without any socks. That's why May 9th is now National Blister Day.

Graffiti: **Computer mating is dater-processing.**

Joke: Q: Why did the chicken cross the highway?
A: To lay it on the line

MAY

Today's Thought: "My uncle's funeral cost five thousand dollars so far. We buried him in a rented tuxedo." -Dave Madden

Observance/Event: The wheel was invented in 50,000 B.C. but the button hole wasn't invented until 1247 so, until then, all those little wheels they sewed on clothes didn't work. It's Hooray for Buttons Day. Here's hoping you have all of yours.

Graffiti: **How do you draw a blank?**

Joke: Q: Why did the Pilgrims' pants always fall down?
A: Because they wore their belt buckles on their hats.

To be sure of hitting the target, shoot first and call whatever you hit the target.

MAY

Today's Thought: "An economic downturn is when they don't have money. A recession is when you don't have money. A depression is when I don't have money." -Sanford Mims

Observance/Event: Today's eye-opening occasion is Stay Up All Night Night, a rather odd event to celebrate, but it does give us the self-serving opportunity to tell you the one about the dyslexic agnostic who had insomnia. He stayed up all night wondering if there really was a dog.

Graffiti: **Never repeat yourself. Never.**

Joke: Q: What does DNA stand for?
A: National Dyslexic Association

MAY

Today's Thought: "I'm for capital punishment. You've got to execute people. How else are they going to learn?" -Mort Sahl

Observance/Event: Satirist and '50s counterculture icon Mort Sahl was born on this day in 1927. So too was the late lovable lush, Foster Brooks, in 1912.

Graffiti: **If you've lost your memory, forget about it.**

Joke: A lawyer wakes up in the hospital after hours of delicate surgery. He looks around the dimly lit room and says, "Hey, Doc, how come the blinds are drawn?"
The doctor answers, "There's a big fire across the street. We didn't want you to think the operation was a failure."

MAY

Today's Thought: "Here's a bumper sticker I'd like to see: 'We are the proud parents of a child whose self-esteem is sufficient that he doesn't need us promoting his minor scholastic achievements on the back of our car.'" -George Carlin

Observance/Event: Iconic humorist George Carlin was born on this day in 1937. It was a difficult birth. In fact, his mother used up all seven words that you can't say on TV.

Graffiti: **Why didn't Noah swat those two mosquitoes?**

Joke: Q: How many drummers does it take to change a light bulb?
A: One... Two, and a-one two three four

MAY

Today's Thought: "I don't think anybody should write his autobiography until after he's dead." -Samuel Goldwyn

Observance/Event: It's National Receptionist Day, a day to recognize the great contributions receptionists make to business. The organizers say that flowers and a champagne toast are in order. Why not have your receptionist call and order some up?...It's also the birthday of humorist and TV host Stephen Colbert, born in 1964.

Graffiti: **Is half of a large intestine a semi-colon?**

Joke: One cannibal says to the other, "You know, I really don't care for my mother-in-law."
The other cannibal replies, "Just eat your vegetables then."

Red meat is not bad for you. Fuzzy green meat is bad for you.

MAY

Today's Thought: "If you don't go to other people's funerals, they won't go to yours." -Clarence Day

Observance/Event: Stars and Stripes Forever Day is the anniversary of the first public performance of John Philip Sousa's famous march in 1897. Straight-laced Philadelphians and President William McKinley alike got down to the sound and boogied the night away.

Graffiti: **Gossip is the knife of the party.**

Joke: The answer is deduce... and the question? What is de lowest card in de deck?

MAY

Today's Thought: "I went to a Chinese bowling alley once. I rented these great shoes, but you weren't allowed to wear them inside." -Wendy Liebman

Observance/Event: It's National Employee Health and Fitness Day, an occasion to focus on the importance of fitness and healthy lifestyles at the worksite. We also hear that exercise kills germs. But how to you get the little buggers to exercise?

Graffiti: **Recycling: The return trip of a bike race**

Joke: A drop-dead gorgeous girl says to the owner of the dress shop, "May I try on that dress in the window?" "Sure," he says, "it'll be great for business!"

MAY

Today's Thought: "Doing nothing is very hard to do. You never know when you're finished." -Leslie Nielsen

Observance/Event: May is "National Mime Month" but mum's the word.

Graffiti: Multiple births are a midwife crisis.

Joke: A husband is on his way out to the store when the wife says, "Please pick up a carton of milk and if they have eggs, get me a dozen."
The husband returns home with 12 cartons of milk.
"Why on earth would you get me 12 cartons of milk?" asks the wife.
"They had eggs."

MAY

Today's Thought: "My father invented the burglar alarm which, unfortunately, was stolen from him." -Victor Borge

Observance/Event: The one who made a fortune off other people's home movies, Bob Saget, the original host of *America's Funnies Home Videos*, was born in Philadelphia on this day in 1956. Another funny TV performer, Craig Ferguson, was born on this day in 1962.

Graffiti: What is a picture of a thousand words worth?

Joke: Q: If a Czar's wife is a Czarina, what would you call their children?
A: Czardines

MAY

Today's Thought: "We need a 12-step group for compulsive talkers. They would call it On Anon Anon."
-Paula Poundstone

Observance/Event: It's Visit Your Relatives Day. Renew family bonds; catch up on how things are going. Visit your relatives before they visit you.

Graffiti: **It's not the bulls or the bears that get you in the stock market...it's the bum steers.**

Joke: As the casket is being carried out after a woman's funeral service, the pallbearers bump into a wall. The husband hears a faint moan, opens the casket and finds out that his wife is still alive!
Ten years later, the woman dies "again" and another funeral is held. After the service, as the casket is being carried toward the door, the husband shouts, "Watch out for the wall!"

MAY

Today's Thought: "I used to date a hoarder, and she broke up with me. That stings extra hard - I'm like the one thing she can get rid of." -Sam Morril

Observance/Event: It's National Police Week (which occurs the calendar week in which May 15 falls). We can't resist telling you the one about toilets being stolen from the police station. The cops investigated and found they had nothing to go on.

Graffiti: **Procrastinators have wait problems.**

Joke: Q: What happened when the elephant sat on the grape?
A: It let out a little wine.

For maximum attention, nothing beats a good mistake.

MAY

20

Today's Thought: "It's a dog-eat-dog world and I'm wearing Milkbone underwear." -Norm, on TV's *Cheers*

Observance/Event: It was closing time for *Cheers* as the final episode of the sitcom aired on this date in 1993 after an 11-year run.

Graffiti: **Easy Street is a blind alley.**

Joke: Barney is meeting with his priest. "Father," he says, "My psychiatrist says I have a split personality, but I still want to get married."
The priest says, "I don't see anything wrong with that, Barney. Who is it that you want to marry?"
"The Murphy twins."

MAY

21

Today's Thought: "Men aren't attracted to me by my mind. They're attracted to me by what I don't mind." -Gypsy Rose Lee

Observance/Event:
To: All interested parties
From: *The Bathroom Joke Almanac*
Subject: National Memo Day
    If you deal daily with a mountain of moronic memos, this is your day to post your own memo concerning the fact that there are too many memos.

Graffiti: **Old basketball players never die; they just dribble away.**

Joke: Then there was a guy who worked at a fire hydrant plant but quit after six months because he could never park near the place.

MAY

Today's Thought: "Government investigations have always contributed more to our amusement than they have to our knowledge." -Will Rodgers

Observance/Event: Note a big day in bathroom history as Dr. Sheffield invented the toothpaste tube in 1892. It's also the anniversary of the day those immortal words, "Please squeeze from the bottom," were first uttered.

Graffiti: **How would you do the YMCA in Chinese?**

Joke: Q: What happened after the termites ate the Chinese restaurant?
A: An hour later, they ate the building next door.

MAY

Today's Thought: "Oh, you hate your job? Why didn't you say so? There's a support group for that. It's called EVERYBODY, and they meet at the bar." -Drew Carey

Observance/Event: Comedian and game show host Drew Carey was born on this day in 1958. It's also Don't Rob a Bank Day. In case you've been considering it, remember the fate of Bonnie & Clyde.

Graffiti: **Dermatologists make rash judgments!**

Joke: Q: How many lawyers does it take to screw in a lightbulb?
A: How many can you afford?

Thanks for explaining the word "many" to me. It means a lot.

MAY

Today's Thought: "The man who sees the consistency in things is a wit; the man who sees the inconsistency in things is a humorist." -G.K. Chesterton

Observance/Event: M*A*S*H*'s Gary Burghoff met his first doctor in 1934 and the man behind Miss Piggy, Frank Oz, was born in 1944.

Graffiti: **A digital clock doesn't run clockwise.**

Joke: A friend of mine went to his doctor because he heard a ringing in his head. The doctor gave him an unlisted ear.

MAY

Today's Thought: "Silly is you in a natural state, and serious is something you have to do until you can get silly again." -Mike Myers

Observance/Event: The very silly comedian, actor and writer Mike Myers was born on this date in 1963.

Graffiti: **If one synchronized swimmer drowns, do the rest have to drown too?**

Joke: Q: Why do fire departments have Dalmatians?
A: To help them find hydrants

A clean house is the sign of a broken computer.

MAY

Today's Thought: "I have a microwave fireplace. You can lie down in front of the fire all night, in eight minutes." -Steven Wright

Observance/Event: Bobcat Goldthwait, known for his acerbic black comedy -"America's one of the finest countries anybody ever stole" - was born on this date in 1962.

Graffiti: **The girl who is easy to get, may be hard to take.**

Joke: "Senator- to show my appreciation I'd like to give you a $60,000 Mercedes from my dealership."
"I can't accept that man, it would be bribery!"
"I could arrange to sell you the car for $50."
"In that case, I'll take two!"

MAY

Today's Thought: "Some tortures are physical and some are mental, but the one that's both is dental." -Ogden Nash

Observance/Event: In 1919, Charles Strite patented the pop-up toaster, an invention that no doubt has made a lot of bread.

Graffiti: **If you want a stable life, marry a horse.**

Joke: Q: What's the opposite of progress?
A: Congress

I've been repeating the same mistakes in life for so long now, I think I'll start calling them traditions.

MAY

Today's Thought: "The reason lightning doesn't strike twice in the same place is that the same place isn't there the second time." -Willie Tyler

Observance/Event: It's Spy Novels Are Splendid Day, on the birthday of author Ian Fleming, whose words were his bond...James Bond.

Graffiti: **If God expected us to be brave, why did he give us legs?**

Joke: Two men are sitting at a bar when one glances at the TV and says, "You know, I got a TV just like that one for my mother-in-law." The guy next to him puts down his glass and says wistfully, "Gee, I'd love to make a deal like that."

MAY

Today's Thought: "I grew up with six brothers. That's how I learned to dance - waiting for the bathroom." -Bob Hope

Observance/Event: Comedian Bob Hope started out on the road to life on this day in 1903.

Graffiti: **24 hours in a day..24 beers in a case... coincidence?**

Joke: Little Johnny's mother wants him to stop sucking his thumb so she tells him if he keeps it up, his stomach is going to get bigger and bigger until it bursts. Later on, Johnny's in the supermarket and sees a very pregnant woman. He can't stop staring at her until the lady finally says, "Look, little boy. You don't know me. You shouldn't be staring like that."
Johnny says, "I may not know you, but I know what you've been doing!"

MAY

Today's Thought: "If there's anyone listening to whom I owe money, I'm prepared to forget it if you are." -Errol Flynn

Observance/Event: The first automobile accident occurred on this date in New York City in 1898. Also, the first personal injury lawyer chased the first ambulance.

Graffiti: To cure the listless feeling, write a list.

Joke: Diner: I think I'll have what the man over there is having.
Waiter: Alright sir, but I don't think he'll be too happy about it.

MAY

Today's Thought: "I walk into rooms and I don't know why I'm there. I'm like, 'Why am I standing in front of the toilet now?'"-Matthew Broderick

Observance/Event: It's Take This Job and Shove It Day, the birthday of Johnny Paycheck. Of course if you say that to your boss, you can pretty much figure your paycheck will go right in the johnny.

Graffiti: Fish get chicken pox on a small scale.

Joke: A grasshopper goes into a bar and orders a beer. The bartender fills the mug and says, "You know, we have a drink here that's named after you."
The grasshopper takes a hit of the beer and says, "You mean to tell me you have a drink called Lester?"

JUNE

Today's Thought: "I think there's a difference between ditzy and dumb. Dumb is just not knowing. Ditzy is having the courage to ask!" -Jessica Simpson

Observance/Event: Funny woman Amy Schumer was born on this day in 1981.

Graffiti: **Humpty Dumpty was pushed.**

Joke: Frick: I just can't lose weight, no matter what.
Frack: Just stop thinking about desserts. Whatever you do, don't think about desserts.
Frick: Do you think I can?
Frack: Piece of cake.

JUNE

Today's Thought: "I like to play chess with bald men in the park, although it's hard to find 32 of them." -Emo Phillips

Observance/Event: It's "Beaver Day"! Jerry Mathers was born on this day in 1948. Sharing a birthday with The Beave, is stand-up comic and actor Dana Carvey, who was born in 1955.

Graffiti: **Confucius say: Ghost who gets lost in fog is mist.**

Joke: A Boston marathoner suffered a sudden spell of dizziness so he stopped for a minute and rested his head between his legs.
Seeing this, a preppy Harvard student asked in very proper fashion, "Have you vertigo?"
The marathoner said, "Yes. Four more miles."

JUNE

Today's Thought: "Remember 'I' before 'E', except in Budweiser." -Professor Irwin Corey

Observance/Event: It's National Repeat Day. It's National Repeat Day.

Graffiti: **Flat feet are arch enemies.**

Joke: Did you hear the one about the guy who went to Las Vegas for some change and rest? The bellhops took the change and the casino took the rest.

JUNE

Today's Thought: "I like to stand near ATM machines, and when somebody types in their pin number, I go, 'Got it!' And then I run away." -Demetri Martin

Observance/Event: Comedian and actor Russell Brand was born on this day in 1975. And this day in 1937 saw the invention of the shopping cart. Since then cranky wheels have been driving everybody buggy.

Graffiti: **Condense soup, not books!**

Joke: Husband: The doctor said to relax, drink carrot juice, followed by a hot bath.
Wife: Did it work?
Husband: I'm not quite sure. I haven't finished drinking the hot bath yet.

JUNE

Today's Thought: "I don't like spinach and I am glad I don't because if I liked it, I'd eat it and I just hate it." -Clarence Darrow

Observance/Event: It's National Bathroom Reading Week. People ask why Johnny can't read. National Bathroom Reading Week asks why can't they read in the johnny?

Graffiti: **If you steal a clean slate, does it go on your record?**

Joke: Q: Why did the Siamese twins move to London?
A: So the other one could drive.

JUNE

Today's Thought: "Thanks to the Interstate Highway System, it is now possible to travel across the country from coast to coast without seeing anything." -Charles Kuralt

Observance/Event: It's National Fragrance Week. This has nothing to do with National Bathroom Reading Week (see June 5th).

Graffiti: **Save the whales. Collect the whole set.**

Joke: Patient: How do my x-rays look, Doc?
Doctor: Well, I just had a consultation and you're going to need surgery.
Patient: A consultation with another specialist?
Doctor: No, with my accountant.

I'm here for whatever you need me to do from the couch.

JUNE

Today's Thought: "All my life, I always wanted to be somebody. Now I see that I should have been more specific." -Jane Wagner

Observance/Event: It's National Chocolate Ice Cream Day- an udderly good time to play *Jeopardy!* The answer is ice cream. And the question… What do you get from an Alaskan cow?

Graffiti: **If a cow laughed, would milk come out of her nose?**

Joke: Woman: Doctor, my husband thinks he's a refrigerator.
Psychiatrist: That seems fairly harmless to me.
Woman: Yes, but he sleeps with his mouth open and the lights keep me awake.

JUNE

Today's Thought: "I really don't think I need buns of steel. I'd be happy with buns of cinnamon." -Ellen DeGeneres

Observance/Event: Comedienne Joan Rivers was born on this date in 1937. She realized she was an unwanted child though, "When I saw that my bath toys were a toaster and a radio."

Graffiti: **Termites never die. They live happily ever rafter.**

Joke: There was a jailbreak and I saw a short prisoner climb up the fence. As he jumped down, he sneered at me and I thought, "Well that's a little condescending."

Everywhere is walking distance if you have the time.

JUNE

Today's Thought: "My grandfather always said, 'Don't watch your money, watch your health.' So one day while I was watching my health, someone stole my money. It was my grandfather." -Jackie Mason

Observance/Event: Comedian Jackie Mason was born Yacov Moshe Maza on this day in 1931.

Graffiti: **Dentures are little white lies.**

Joke: "Waiter! There's a fly in my soup!"
"That's funny. There were two of them when I left the kitchen."

JUNE

Today's Thought: "My father once told me all about the birds and the bees. The liar. I went steady with a woodpecker till I was twenty-one." -Bob Hope

Observance/Event: We admit to milking a lot of cheesy occasions in this book but this one is no bull. June is National Dairy Month.

Graffiti: **An astronomer is a night watchman.**

Joke: Q: What do you call two thousand pounds of Chinese soup?
A: Won Ton

Never laugh at your girlfriend's choices. You're one of them.

JUNE

Today's Thought: "If a woman has to choose between a fly ball and saving an infant's life, she will choose to save the infant's life without even considering if there are men on base." -Dave Barry

Observance/Event: It's Corn On The Cob Day. Here's some corn for you: What did the corn say when he got complimented?... Aww, shucks!

Graffiti: **I don't suffer from insanity. I enjoy every minute of it.**

Joke: A guy walks into the doctor's office. He has a banana stuck in one of his ears, a corn cob in the other ear, and a carrot stuck in one nostril. He says, "Doc, this is horrible. What's wrong with me?" The doctor says, "Well, the first thing you need to do is to eat more sensibly."

JUNE

Today's Thought: "When your friends begin to flatter you on how young you look, it's a sure sign you're getting old." -Mark Twain

Observance/Event: He was born on February 29, but the folks at D.C. Entertainment decided to give him his very own special occasion on this day and so today is Superman Day.

Graffiti: **There's no future in time travel.**

Joke: Five-year-old Johnny was dressed in a Superman cape when he went with his mother for a pre-school interview with his teacher. The teacher asked Johnny his name and he said, "Superman."
The teacher smiled, repeated the question and Johnny repeated, "Superman."
The teacher then said, "No, Johnny. Really. Whisper your name in my ear."
Johnny whispered in her ear, "Clark Kent."

JUNE

Today's Thought: "Too bad that all the people who know how to run the country are busy driving taxicabs and cutting hair." -George Burns

Observance/Event: It's Sewing Machine Day in honor of its invention, but we prefer the yarns of comedian Alonzo Bodden who was born on this day in 1962.

Graffiti: Death is life's way of telling you you've been fired.

Joke: Q: What did the ancient Romans yell on the golf course? A: "IV!"

JUNE

Today's Thought: "If at first you don't succeed, stay away from skydiving." -Milton Berle

Observance/Event: Flag Day commemorates the day in 1777 when John Adams introduced a resolution to make the Stars 'n' Stripes our nation's official flag. Actually, Old Glory was his second choice but Abigail refused to donate a pair of her pantaloons for the cause.

Graffiti: Poets marry for better or verse.

Joke: A guy comes home and finds his wife, a noted psychic, standing at the front door with a baseball bat in hand. "You no good louse," she growled, "and just where were you until 3 a.m. tomorrow morning?"

JUNE

Today's Thought: "Start every day off with a smile and get it over with." -W.C. Fields

Observance/Event: It's Smile Power Day. And it's also the birthday of comedian/actor Jim Belushi, who was born in 1954.

Graffiti: **Draft beer, not people.**

Joke: Father: "Son, do you realize that when Abraham Lincoln was your age he was already reading books, studying to become an attorney?"
Son: "You're absolutely right dad, and by the time he was your age, he was already president."

JUNE

Today's Thought: "We should be grateful for subways. At least they've taken crime off of the streets." -Will Jordan

Observance/Event: Here's one you'll get a charge out of- it's National Electricity Day- but remember, that's no excuse to get lit.

Graffiti: **Ever stop to think, and forget to start again?**

Joke: Husband: "Why don't we go home early and make some whoopee? They say it's very good for the flu."
Wife: "But I haven't got the flu."
Husband: "So- you never heard of preventive medicine?"

If I had a dollar for every girl that found me unattractive, they'd eventually find me attractive.

JUNE

Today's Thought: "When I was a kid I got no respect. I told my mother, 'I'm gonna run away from home.' She said, 'On your mark...'" -Rodney Dangerfield

Observance/Event: Joe Piscopo felt the burn for the first time as the doctor slapped his gluteus maximus on this day in 1951. A few years later, he went back and slapped the doctor.

Graffiti: **"Popcorn" is when fathers tell jokes.**

Joke: Did you hear the one about the farmer who planted cabbages and razor blades? He was hoping to raise cole slaw.

JUNE

Today's Thought: "My biggest worry is that when I'm dead and gone, my wife will sell my fishing gear for what I said I paid for it." -Koos Brandt

Observance/Event: Go Fishing Day is celebrated today, reminding us of some good ol' hook, line and stinkers. Check it out below.

Graffiti: **Mrs. Paul's Fish Sticks. Does Yours?**

Joke: A couple of Eskimos went fishing on an extremely frigid day. They lit a fire in the bottom of their kayak to warm up, but moments later the blaze raged out of control and their boat sank.
The moral of the story: You can't have your kayak and heat it, too.

You're so ugly, when your mom dropped you off at school she got a fine for littering.

JUNE

Today's Thought: "I'm not turned on by baseball. My idea of a relief pitcher is one that's filled with martinis."
-Dean Martin

Observance/Event: Cheers! It's officially Martini Day- and here's a conversation starter for your cocktail hour: Albert Einstein would never tell a German bartender his name - because every time he did he got a beer.

Graffiti: **Count Dracula, Your Bloody Mary is ready.**

Joke: An extremely inebriated fellow walks into a bar, climbs on top of a barstool and shouts, "All lawyers are idiots!"
A guy down at the end of the bar says, "I resent that remark."
The drunk yells back, "Why, are you a lawyer?"
"No, I'm an idiot."

JUNE

Today's Thought: "The trouble with eating Italian food is that five or six days later, you're hungry again."
-George Miller

Observance/Event: It's Ice Cream Soda Day so celebrate with a few scoops of Good Humor!

Graffiti: **Support the Marcel Marceau Foundation because a mime is a terrible thing to waste.**

Joke: Wally took his mother-in-law by complete surprise when he presented her with a delicately scented, beautifully wrapped birthday gift. She unwrapped the present and opened the box to find a beautiful pair of earrings and a loaded handgun.
"Why, Wally, these are really gorgeous, but why the gun?"
"That's to pierce your ears with."

JUNE

Today's Thought: "A zebra does not change its spots." -Al Gore

Observance/Event: It's Selfie Day, though the publishers of this book don't recommend you mark the occasion just now, considering your likely whereabouts. Meanwhile, comedian Jim Breuer was born on this date in 1967.

Graffiti: **Change is inevitable, except from a vending machine.**

Joke: A sports car and a Mack truck get into a fender-bender on the I-10 in L.A.
The incensed sports car driver jumps up on the truck's running board, holds his hands out at an angle and screams, "Karate!"
The truck driver flattens him with a wallop to the head and yells, "Monkey wrench!"

JUNE

Today's Thought: "Everything is funny as long as it's happening to somebody else." -Will Rogers

Observance/Event: For police everywhere, this is a high hole-y day. The doughnut was invented in 1847.

Graffiti: **You never realize how short a month is, until you pay alimony.**

Joke: Q: What do you get when you cross a crocodile with a sausage?
A: A crockabaloney

If you can smile when things go wrong, you have someone in mind to blame.

JUNE

Today's Thought: "Maybe that's why I like animals. Woof. Moo. Quack. They tell it like it is."
-Frank Barone, *Everybody Loves Raymond*

Observance/Event: It's Cosmic Patience Day, a time to ponder how long we will have to wait for an answer to an interplanetary message sent in 1974 (probably about the same amount of time it takes your cable company to answer the phone).

Graffiti: **Be different: Conform.**

Joke: I went to paint a store once and they had handicapped parking spaces for people who were color-blind.

JUNE

Today's Thought: "Just remember, when you're over the hill, you begin to pick up speed." -Charles Schulz

Observance/Event: The modern era of "flying saucers" began in 1947 as Kenneth Arnold reported a formation of UFO's over Mt. Rainer, WA. Previously, the only reports of flying saucers came from nudists who spilled hot tea in their laps.

Graffiti: **"Criminal Lawyer" is a redundancy.**

Joke: Q: Where can you find a lawyer who doesn't lie, cheat or steal?
A: In the cemetery

When I call a family meeting, I turn off the house Wifi and wait for them all to come running.

JUNE

Today's Thought: "Some of you are really smart. You know who you are. Some of you are really thick. Unfortunately, you don't know who you are." -Ricky Gervais

Observance/Event: English comedian Ricky Gervais was born on this day in 1961.

Graffiti: **How come there are no "B" batteries?**

Joke: Patient: Doc, I have some dimes stuck in my ear.
Doctor: How long have they been there?
Patient: About six months.
Doctor: Why didn't you come sooner?
Patient: I didn't need the money.

JUNE

Today's Thought: "Fun is like life insurance. The older you get, the more it costs." -Kin Hubbard

Observance/Event: It's Clean Out Your Medicine Cabinet Day. *The Bathroom Joke Almanac* reminds you to safely dispose of those unwanted medications; Uncle Charlie's Tooth Powder from 1957, Aunt Emma's secret ointment for "The Miseries" and that old can of hair spray-on you once mistook for deodorant.

Graffiti: **Nothing political is correct.**

Joke: In downtown Philadelphia, a tourist stops to ask a shop owner how far it is to the Liberty Bell.
"The way you're going, 25,000 miles."

JUNE

Today's Thought: "There are too many comedians today. Soon the government will pay you not to do stand-up the same way they pay you not to grow wheat." -Rita Rudner

Observance/Event: It's National Fink Day for rat finks, dirty finks and anybody named Fink.

Graffiti: **To err is human, to moo bovine.**

Joke: Doctor: How did you get that terrible gash in your ear?
Man: I bit myself.
Doctor: It's anatomically impossible for a man to bite himself on the ear.
Man: No, it's not. I was standing on a chair.

JUNE

Today's Thought: "Some lawyers are like laundries. They lose your shirt but still take you to the cleaners." -Larry Wilde

Observance/Event: Comic/producer Mel Brooks was born Melvin Kaminsky on this day in 1928.

Graffiti: **Every time your ship comes in, the government unloads it.**

Joke: An absent-minded guy comes home from work.
His wife says, "Where did you leave your umbrella?"
He says, "Gee, I don't know."
She says, "Well, when did you become aware that it was missing?"
He says, "Well, when it stopped raining, I reached up to close it and it was gone."

JUNE

Today's Thought: "About the time we think we can make ends meet, someone moves the ends." -Herbert Hoover

Observance/Event: A big day for armchair quarterbacks and couch potatoes everywhere...the television remote control made its TV debut in 1964. Today's birthday boy is comedian Richard Lewis, who was born in 1947.

Graffiti: **Unemployment isn't working.**

Joke: Q: What do you get if you cross a pigeon and a general?
A: A military coo.

JUNE

Today's Thought: "College is the best time of your life. Where else are your parents going to spend thousands of dollars a year just for you to go to a strange town and get drunk every night?" -David Wood

Observance/Event: Comedian/actor David Alan Grier's first appearance on this planet was on this date in 1956.

Graffiti: **Those who indulge, bulge.**

Joke: A man walks into an Irish bar with an alligator on a leash.
"Do you serve Americans here?" he asked.
"We sure do," replied the bartender.
"Great. Then I'll have a daiquiri and my 'gator will have an American."

JULY

Today's Thought: "I don't want to be immortal through my work. I want to be immortal through not dying." -Woody Allen

Observance/Event: On this date in 1952, Dan Akroyd was definitely not yet ready for prime time as he was born in Ottawa.

Graffiti: **Warning: Dates on calendar are closer than they appear.**

Joke: Did you hear the one about the woman who made a fortune cleaning computers? Her slogan was, "I do Windows."

JULY

Today's Thought: "There's a television commercial where a customer in a drug store never heard of Preparation H. Where has he had his head?" -Gallagher

Observance/Event: July is Read An Almanac Month to make people aware of what wonderful, entertaining, enriching, fabulous, absolutely indispensable things almanacs are. Modesty prevents us from saying any more. Don't curb your enthusiasm just yet, though, because it's also time to celebrate Larry David's birthday. He was born on this date in 1947.

Graffiti: **Overweight is living beyond your seams.**

Joke: Then there was the guy who got fired from the calendar factory just for taking a day off.

JULY

Today's Thought: "Smartness runs in my family. When I went to school, I was so smart my teacher was in my class for five years." -Gracie Allen

Observance/Event: The "Dog Days" begin today. Despite reports to the contrary, there's no truth to the rumor that the period of summer and swelter was so-named from the day it was so hot that a dog was seen chasing a cat and they were both walking.

Graffiti: **A closed mouth gathers no foot.**

Joke: Q: How do pigs round the bases?
A: They go "wee-wee-wee-wee" all the way home.

JULY

Today's Thought: "It's Fourth of July weekend, or, as I call it, Exploding Christmas." -Stephen Colbert

Observance/Event: Not only was America born on this day but also one of its favorite humorists, Neil Simon, who began his first draft of life back in 1927.

Graffiti: **The doctor may be a quack, but you still can't duck his bills.**

Joke: Two elephants are talking, when one says to the other, "I don't care what they say, I can't remember a thing."

Laziness is when a person doesn't fake that he's working.

JULY

Today's Thought: "Never, under any circumstances, take a sleeping pill and a laxative on the same night." -Dave Barry

Observance/Event: News flush! Just when you thought the fireworks were over, comes this item: July is National Baked Bean Month!

Graffiti: **It's not whether you win or lose, it's how you place the blame.**

Joke: Sid: My shop got burglarized last night and the thieves got everything!
Stu: That's terrible.
Sid: Not as bad as if they had broken in the night before. I just finished marking everything down 50%.

JULY

Today's Thought: "Procrastination is the art of keeping up with yesterday." -Don Marquis

Observance/Event: The weekend following July Fourth is National Nude Weekend. It's also National Stay Away From Wicker Furniture Days... Funnyman Kevin Hart was born on this date in 1979.

Graffiti: **Adam loved Eve — who else?**

Joke: And then there was the boxer whose tombstone read, "You can stop counting. I'm not getting up."

Turning vegan is a big missed steak.

JULY

Today's Thought: "Pie can't compete with cake. Put candles in a cake, it's a birthday cake. Put candles in a pie, and somebody's drunk in the kitchen." -Jim Gaffigan

Observance/Event: They're lighting the candles for Jim Gaffigan's birthday cake today. The comedian was born on this date in 1966.

Graffiti: **Kangaroos drink hopscotch**

Joke: Q: What does a mobster buried in cement eventually become?
A: A hardened criminal

JULY

Today's Thought: "I talk to myself because I like dealing with a better class of people." -Jackie Mason

Observance/Event: The Declaration of Independence was read publicly for the first time on this date in 1776 in Philadelphia. By the way, you know where it was signed, don't you? At the bottom.

Graffiti: **Henry Ford's diary is an autobiography.**

Joke: Riley was speeding down the road at seventy miles per hour. He was pulled over by a cop who said, "Do you know the speed limit is fifty five miles per hour?"
"Yes, officer," replied Riley, looking as innocent as possible, "but I wasn't going to be out that long."

The best things in life are free - plus shipping and handling.

JULY

Today's Thought: "Sometimes I think the surest sign that intelligent life exists elsewhere in the universe is that none of it has tried to contact us." -Bill Watterson

Observance/Event: On this day in 1872, John Blondel invented the world's first donut cutter. Law enforcement officers everywhere plan to give him a 21-dunk salute.

Graffiti: **Dolphins have a porpoise in life.**

Joke: The sergeant scolded the private, "You failed to show up for camouflage class yesterday!"
The private responded, "And how do you know that, sir?"

JULY

Today's Thought: "I'm desperately trying to figure out why kamikaze pilots wore helmets." -Dave Edison

Observance/Event: It's Lady Godiva Day, commemorating her famous horseback ride through Coventry while totally naked, circa 1040. (This event gave new meaning to the term "riding bareback".)

Graffiti: **Where there's a will, there's a relative.**

Joke: A woman walking down Fifth Avenue is accosted by an animal rights protestor.
"How dare you wear that fur coat? Do you know how much that poor animal suffered just so you could wear that thing?"
"Oh," replied the woman, "so you know my husband?"

You're not completely useless. You can always serve as a bad example.

JULY

Today's Thought: "Only one man in a thousand is a leader of men- the other 999 follow women." -Groucho Marx

Observance/Event: The United States Marines began their long march from the halls of Montezuma to the shores of Tripoli, on this date back in 1798. Of course, after that Montezuma run-in, their motto was, "We're looking for a few good men's rooms."

Graffiti: **Ghosts live on dead ends.**

Joke: Terrorists raided the annual attorneys' convention in New York and held all the lawyers hostage. They threatened that until their demands were met, they'd release a lawyer every hour.

JULY

Today's Thought: "We owe a lot to Thomas Edison. If it wasn't for him, we'd be watching television by candlelight." -Milton Berle

Observance/Event: Milton Berle, who was "Uncle Miltie" and "Mr. Television" during TV's golden age, took to the world's stage for the first time on this day in 1908.

Graffiti: **A fortune teller has medium prices.**

Joke: Hospital scene-
Distraught mother: Doctor, doctor! My son's been run over by a steamroller! Where is he?
Doctor: Ahh, yes...the steamroller victim. He's in rooms 210, 211 and 212.

JULY

Today's Thought: "If the formula for water is H_2O, is the formula for an ice cube H_2O squared?" -Lily Tomlin

Observance/Event: It's Embrace Your Geekness Day, so go ahead, show off your nerdiness. By the way, you want fries with that? It's also French Fries Day.

Graffiti: **How long a minute is depends on which side of the bathroom door you're on.**

Joke: Woman: Help! My house is on fire! Come quick!
Dispatcher: OK, calm down. Now, how do we get there?
Woman: Whatsamatter? Don't you have that big red truck anymore?

JULY

Today's Thought: "To my wife double parking means on top of another car." -Dave Barry

Observance/Event: The Prince of Pratfalls, ex-President Gerald R. Ford, was born today in 1913.

Graffiti: **A chimney sweeper's job soots him.**

Joke: An inebriated mathematician arrives home at three in the morning. His highly agitated wife yells, "You're late. You said you'd be home no later than 11:45!"
The mathematician answers, "My dear, I am precisely on time. I believe I said I'd be home by a quarter of twelve."

The trouble with unemployment is that the minute you wake up in the morning you're on the job.

JULY

Today's Thought: "The early bird gets the worm. The early worm… gets eaten." -Norman Ralph Augustine

Observance/Event: It's National Gummi Worm Day, quite naturally promoted by the candymakers, who bring you this joke as well: What do you call a worm who lost his dentures? …A gummy worm

Graffiti: **Sir Lancelot's horse was a knight-mare.**

Joke: Husband: Doctor! Doctor! My wife is in labor and she keeps screaming, "Shouldn't, wouldn't, couldn't!"
Doctor: Don't be alarmed. She's just having contractions.

JULY

Today's Thought: "You might be a redneck if your TV gets 512 channels but you go outside to use the bathroom." -Jeff Foxworthy

Observance/Event: Comic actor Will Ferrell was born on this day in 1967.

Graffiti: **Behind every successful man, is an IRS agent!**

Joke: "Doctor, we've got an emergency! My baby just swallowed all my golf tees!"
"I'll be there at once."
"What should I do 'til you get here, Doc?"
"Practice your putting."

When I get naked in the bathroom, the shower usually gets turned on.

JULY

Today's Thought: "We had the Greatest Generation, the Boomers, Generation X, Generation Y, and now: Generation Text." -Greg Tamblyn

Observance/Event: The late great funnylady Phyllis Diller came into the world on this day in 1917 and like she said, "I was so ugly, the doctor spanked my mother."

Graffiti: **If you wanted control, you should have married your remote!**

Joke: Then there was the company president who was in the hospital recovering from surgery. He received a get-well card from the board of directors who wrote, "We wish you a speedy recovery…by a vote of four to three."

JULY

Today's Thought: "The average dog is a nicer person than the average person." -Andy Rooney

Observance/Event: Comedic legend Red Skelton and his alter egos, Freddie the Freeloader and Clem Kadiddlehopper, were born on this day in 1913.

Graffiti: **Money isn't everything but it keeps you in touch with the kids.**

Joke: Fred and Ethel were having a discussion about family finances. Finally, the wife lost her temper. "If it weren't for my money, this house wouldn't be here!"
The husband replied, "Listen, Ethel, if it weren't for your money, I wouldn't be here."

JULY

Today's Thought: "I have little feet because nothing grows in the shade." -Dolly Parton

Observance/Event: It's Bloomer Day, marking the day in 1848 when Amelia Bloomer introduced the garment that was to bear her name.

Graffiti: **Fortune tellers have a ball.**

Joke: Personnel Interviewer: Are you a "yes" man?
Job Applicant: Maybe...

JULY

Today's Thought: "My teacher told me that today is the first day of the rest of my life. That explains why I didn't do yesterday's homework." -Lorne Elliot

Observance/Event: It's Creative Ice Cream Flavor Day. Put Baskin Robbins to shame. Let your imagination run wild. How about Zinc Oxide Mocha SPF#15? Or maybe Banana Nut Oat Bran or a nice Spinach-Bubble gum sundae?

Graffiti: **Dieters are people who are thick and tired of it.**

Joke:
He: "I accidentally swallowed my watch."
She: "Does it hurt?"
He: "Only when I try to wind it."

JULY

21

Today's Thought: "Baseball is a sport in which men who rested all winter need weeks of spring training for a summer of playing games." -Doug Larson

Observance/Event: Comedic actor Don Knotts was born in 1924; Robin Williams opened in 1952; and Jon Lovitz came into the world in 1957…no lie.

Graffiti: Confucius say: If people string you along, you become real yo-yo.

Joke: A drunk goes up to an elevator and hits the 'down' button. The door opens, he steps in, but there's no elevator. He plummets twelve stories to the bottom of the shaft. He gets up, brushes himself off and says, "Maybe I should've pushed 'up'."

JULY

22

Today's Thought: "No wonder why golf is a sport in which tempers grow very thin; it's the only game in which players are teed off when they begin." -George O. Ludcke

Observance/Event: It's Hammock Day- a day to have fun lying.

Graffiti: Environmental activists are ecomaniacs!

Joke: A guest from Montreal was staying at a little bed and breakfast near Toronto. He called down to the clerk and asked for some pepper.
"Will that be black pepper or white pepper sir?" asked his host.
A bit annoyed, the guest answered, "Toilette Pepper!"

My grandfather has the heart of a lion and a lifetime ban at the zoo.

JULY

Today's Thought: "Cats have nine lives. Which makes them ideal for experimentation." -Jimmy Carr

Observance/Event: It's Gorgeous Grandma Day... While we're on the topic of grandmothers, what do you call having your grandma on speed dial? ...Instagram

Graffiti: **Honk if you like noise pollution!**

Joke: Frick: I called my psychiatrist and told him that I thought I had kleptomania.
Frack: What did he say?
Frick: He told me to take something for it.

JULY

Today's Thought: "The phrase 'The Melting Pot' used to mean the United States of America. Now it means you put the wrong container in the microwave." -Robert Orben

Observance/Event: Instant coffee was invented on this day in 1938. Unfortunately, it would be many years before they cracked the formula for hot water.

Graffiti: **Middle Age: When your hairline's going up and your gum line's going down.**

Joke: The answer is Pandemonium... and the question?
What do they call a retirement hi-rise for pandas?

People say money is not the key to happiness, but I always figured if you had enough money, you can have a key made.

JULY

Today's Thought: "Always borrow money from a pessimist. He won't expect it back." -Oscar Wilde

Observance/Event: The lowest natural temperature ever recorded was set in Antarctica in 1983. The thermometer reached 129 degrees below zero. (It was so cold, lawyers had their hands in their own pockets!)

Graffiti: A chef is a man for all seasonings.

Joke: A man told his doctor that he suspected he had a split personality so the doctor charged him double!

JULY

Today's Thought: "When I was born, I was so surprised, I couldn't talk for a year and a half." -Gracie Allen

Observance/Event: Two legendary ladies of laughter were born on this day: Gracie Allen in 1906 and Vivian Vance in 1912.

Graffiti: By the time you're old enough to be nostalgic, your memory's too short.

Joke: A guy walks into a lumberyard and asks for some two-by-fours. The clerk asks, "How long do you need them?" The guy answers, "A long time. We're gonna build a house."

JULY

Today's Thought: "The second day of a diet is always easier than the first. By the second day, you're off of it." -Jackie Gleason

Observance/Event: This it it- an occasion for the truly sedentary. The event speaks for itself. It's Take Your Houseplant For A Walk Day!

Graffiti: The leading cause of death in lab mice is research.

Joke: Little Johnny's riding with his mother when they pull up to a stoplight alongside another car. Johnny peers over and can't believe his eyes as he sees a totally naked woman in the driver's seat. "Well, will you look at that, Ma!" Johnny says. "That lady's not wearing a seat belt!"

JULY

Today's Thought: "Nothing in fine print is ever good news." -Andy Rooney

Observance/Event: One of Hollywood's most famous comedy scriptwriters/producers, Norman Lear (*All in the Family, Maude*), was born on this date in 1922.

Graffiti: Earthquake predictors are faultfinders.

Joke: The scene is at the side of the road.
Driver: What seems to be the trouble officer?
Cop: Bad news sir. Your wife fell out of the car ten miles back.
Driver: Oh, thank goodness. I thought I was going deaf!

I don't have a solution, but I do admire the problem.

JULY

Today's Thought: "I had a lazy eye as a kid, and it gradually spread to my whole body." -Tom Cotter

Observance/Event: It's Rainy Day in Waynesburg, Pennsylvania, where legend has it that rain will fall on this date as it has for most years. In honor of the occasion, we bring you this groaner: What's worse than raining cats and dogs? Hailing taxis.

Graffiti: **Genetic engineering is heir styling.**

Joke: Q: What do you get if you tie two bikes together?
A: Siamese Schwinns

JULY

Today's Thought: "The worst time to have a heart attack is during a game of charades." -Demetri Martin

Observance/Event: It's Father-in-Law Day, also known as Another Greeting Card Companies Holiday Day.

Graffiti: **How come there are no father-in-law jokes?**

Joke: Doctor: Now take this medication only with meals. That'll be $200.
Patient: But Doc, I'm broke. I haven't eaten in a week.
Doctor: Great- then the pills will last a lot longer.

Why does it feel like time slows down during the day when you're at work and rapidly speeds up at night when you get home?

JULY

Today's Thought: "I wouldn't mind being the last man on Earth…just to see if all those girls were telling me the truth."
-Ronnie Shakes

Observance/Event: Henry Perky patented Shredded Wheat on this day in 1893. It was an accidental discovery. Actually, he was trying to perfect the world's smallest hay-baler.

Graffiti: **For sale: Ex-wife. Take over payments.**

Joke: Job applicant: Yes, I am a good lumberjack. Ever heard of Sahara Forest?
Foreman: You mean the Sahara Desert?
Job Applicant: Sure, that's what they call it now.

AUGUST

Today's Thought: "I'm going to change my name on Facebook to 'Benefits', so that when you add me, it will say, 'You are now friends with benefits.'" -Ben Kreismer

Observance/Event: Today we celebrate World Wide Web Day- a day of online fun at your fingertips. While you're at it, do you know why it took the Philadelphia Phillies such a long time to get a website? …They couldn't string together three w's.

Graffiti: **Possessiveness is a state of mine.**

Joke: Frick: I rented a summer place in the Hamptons. It's right on the beach.
Frack: Is it a big house?
Frick: Big? Four stories…five when the tide goes out.

AUGUST

Today's Thought: "If I could drop dead right now, I'd be the happiest man alive!" -Pete Townshend

Observance/Event: In 1892, Charles Wheeler patented the first escalator. A hillbilly friend of his was the first person to ride on it. Unfortunately, there was a power outage and the poor guy was trapped for hours.

Graffiti: Schizophrenia beats drinking alone.

Joke: Two goats are eating at the town dump. One goat finds a roll of film and starts munching on it. The other goat says, "How's the film?"
The first goat responds, "I liked the book better."

AUGUST

Today's Thought: "At 82, I feel like a 20-year-old but, unfortunately, there's never one around." -Milton Berle

Observance/Event: It's National Grab Some Nuts Day but if that's, well, a little too nutty for you, here's some more food for thought- it's also Watermelon Day.

Graffiti: General Custer was the first to wear an arrow shirt.

Joke: Two guys are out hunting at the lake when one of them bags a duck. Instantly, his Golden Retriever walks on top of the lake to fetch the duck.
"That's unbelievable!" his hunting buddy says. "Your dog just walked on water! Amazing!!"
"Ah, not really," says the first hunter. "He can't swim."

AUGUST

Today's Thought: "Assume nothing. Inside every dumb blonde, there may be a very smart brunette." -Ann Landers

Observance/Event: It's okay to get excited, but don't pop your cork. Champagne was invented on this day in 1693.

Graffiti: **How come 'lisp' has an 's' in it?**

Joke: Did you hear the one about the movie theater owner who passed away? Services were held at 2:30, 4:40, and 6:45.

AUGUST

Today's Thought: "I don't believe in an afterlife, although I am bringing a change of underwear." -Woody Allen

Observance/Event: Today we literally observe an unmentionable occasion. It's National Underwear Day. This, of course, begs the unanswerable question: Why does Superman wear his underwear outside his pants?

Graffiti: **A bird in the hand is better than one over your head.**

Joke: Then there was the tattoo artist who was fired for having designs on his clients.

The depressing thing about tennis is that no matter how good I get, I'll never be as good as a wall.

AUGUST

Today's Thought: "A salesman is a fellow with a smile on his face, a shine on his shoes and a lousy territory." -George Globel

Observance/Event: Today in 1911, "Waaaahhhh!" was first heard from Lucille Ball.

Graffiti: **Smoking cures weight problems...eventually.**

Joke: A man takes his Basset Hound to the vet and says, "My dog is cross-eyed. Is there anything you can do for him?"
The vet picks the dog up and examines his eyes. Finally he says, "I'm going to have to put him down."
"What!? Just because he's cross-eyed?"
"No," replied the vet, "because he's really, really heavy."

AUGUST

Today's Thought: "You know you had a good night when you have to Google map yourself in the morning to find out where the hell you are." -Harry Roy

Observance/Event: It's Sneak Zucchini onto Your Neighbor's Porch Night- the only way to get rid of that bumper crop of zucchini that's taking over your yard. Be careful not to trespass, however, or your neighbor might press charges and you'll end up in a squash court.

Graffiti: **If the No. 2 pencil is the most popular, how come it's not No. 1?**

Joke: People are choosing cremation over traditional burial. It shows that they're thinking outside the box.

AUGUST

Today's Thought: "If I die before my cat, I want a little of my ashes put in his food so I can live inside him." -Drew Barrymore

Observance/Event: It's International Cat Day. And now for your feline funny: What do you feed an invisible cat? ...Evaporated milk.

Graffiti: **Here I sit my dignity tarnished. The toilet seat was freshly varnished.**

Joke: "Well, I got good news and bad news at the doctor's today."
"What's the good news?"
"He found out what I had."
"And the bad news?"
"He took every penny of it."

AUGUST

Today's Thought: "I buy books on suicide at bookstores. You can't get them at the library, because people don't return them." -Kevin Nealon

Observance/Event: The first full week of August is National Smile Week and on this day in 1944, Smokey Bear was born. All of which means that today, you should grin and bear it.

Graffiti: **Confucius say: Man who fall in vat of molten glass make spectacle of self.**

Joke: The answer is intense... and the question?
Where do campers sleep?

I am known at the gym as the "before picture."

AUGUST

Today's Thought: "If God had wanted us to plant gardens, he wouldn't have created supermarkets." -James Dent

Observance/Event: August is National Psychic Month, but then, you already knew that, didn't you?

Graffiti: **Prune juice makes the going great.**

Joke: A guy visits a nudist colony. He sees a man with a beard down to his knees walking by. The visitor asks, "Who's that?" "Oh, that's Fuzzy! Someone has to go out for the bagels and coffee."

AUGUST

Today's Thought: "There are two types of people in the world, the good and bad. The good sleep better, but the bad seem to enjoy the waking hours much more." -Woody Allen

Observance/Event: It's Presidential Joke Day, the anniversary of President Reagan's 1984 remarks about bombing Russia that were inadvertently picked up by live mikes. Feel free to relieve any frustration you may have regarding the Chef Executive- after all, the rest of the year, the joke's on you!

Graffiti: **Butchers make both ends meat.**

Joke: Q: How does Moses make coffee?
A: Hebrews it.

The difference between in-laws and outlaws? Outlaws are wanted.

AUGUST

Today's Thought: "I have to exercise in the morning before my brain figures out what I'm doing." -Marsha Doble

Observance/Event: Scorch that skin and heat your hide- it's Get A Tan Day, celebrated annually on the birthday of George Hamilton.

Graffiti: **A sleeping bag is a nap sack.**

Joke: Knock, knock.
Who's there?
Effervescent.
Effervescent who?
Effervescent for wine, women and song, I'd be a pretty good husband.

AUGUST

Today's Thought: "If there are no stupid questions, then what kind of questions do stupid people ask? Do they get smart just in time to ask questions?" -Scott Adams

Observance/Event: It's International Lefthanders Day and remember this adage: If the right side of the mind controls the left side of the body, this means only left-handed people are in their right minds.

Graffiti: **To err is human- To blame it on somebody else is even more human.**

Joke: Q: What do you call a baby monkey?
A: A chimp off the old block.

A friend of mine tried to annoy me with bird puns, but I soon realized that toucan play at that game.

AUGUST

14

Today's Thought: "Facebook should have a limit on the amount of times you can change your relationship status. After three, it should default to 'unstable'." -Robin Kreismer

Observance/Event: The wild and crazy Steve Martin ended his nine-month engagement at his first venue, The Mother's Womb, in Waco, Texas, on this day in 1945.

Graffiti: **Be true to your teeth and they won't be false to you.**

Joke: Q: What's the difference between one yard and two yards?
A: Usually, a fence.

AUGUST

15

Today's Thought: "Sometimes I'm afraid of bears. Sometimes I'm not. I must be bipolar." -Peter Sasso

Observance/Event: It's National Relaxation Day. We'd tell you more about it, but hey, we're observing it too.

Graffiti: **Give a dandelion an inch and it takes over a yard.**

Joke: Son: Well Dad, I finally got my merit badge.
Father: That's great, Son. What was it for?
Son: For fixing bicycle horns.
Father: They give merit badges for fixing bicycle horns?
Son: Sure. In fact, the Boy Scouts' motto is "Beep Repaired."

Just when you think you can make ends meet, somebody moves the ends.

AUGUST

Today's Thought: "If you believe there is a solution, you're part of the problem." -George Carlin

Observance/Event: It's Joe Miller's Joke Day, commemorating the 18th century English actor who inspired the very first joke book (which is not only a historical and precedent-setting publication, it's also in the public domain so we can steal the author blind!).

Graffiti: **William Tell wore contact lenses.**

Joke: Two cannibals were scavenging through a garbage can. One of them came across a discarded *Sports Illustrated* swimsuit issue and said to the other, "Look at this menu!"

AUGUST

Today's Thought: "Few people think more than two or three times a year. I have made an international reputation for myself thinking once or twice a week." -George Bernard Shaw

Observance/Event: On the Saturday nearest Woodstock Weekend, the 15th to the 17th, all ex-flower children celebrate Hippie Day. It's a happening, man- far out, dig it. Get out your old groovy jeans and hope your old groovy still fits into them. Peace.

Graffiti: **The only friend you can buy for money is a dog.**

Joke: Q: How did the girl break up with the tractor driver?
A: She sent him a John Deere letter.

AUGUST

18

Today's Thought: "A hair in the head is worth two in the brush." -Oliver Herford

Observance/Event: It's Bad Poetry Day so dabble in some iambic pentameter or whip up some haiku.

Graffiti: **Cookbooks are full of stirring passages.**

Joke: A guy comes running from the woods of Montana, yelling, "I just shot an elk!"
One of the locals says to him, "Are you sure? I never saw any elk here."
"Absolutely, there's a member card in his wallet."

AUGUST

19

Today's Thought: "The truly great things happen when a genius is alone. This is true especially among golfers." -J.R. Coulson

Observance/Event: It's National Aviation Day and Go to The Track Day, so combine the events- take off and go to the track.

Graffiti: **Humpty Pumpty is just a shell of his former self.**

Joke: Herb and Harry were teeing off early one summer's day when the usual tranquility of the golf course was shattered by the siren of an ambulance racing to the maternity hospital atop a nearby hill.
"Somebody's getting a big surprise today," remarked Harry.
"I'll say," replied Herb as he lined up his putt. "When I left this morning, my wife's contractions were still at least an hour apart."

AUGUST

Today's Thought: "Why is it when you're seven today is forever and tomorrow is never; but when you're 70, tomorrow's yesterday before you knew it was today?"
-Sue Jane Purcell

Observance/Event: If your 'do doesn't, if your style is vile or your cut is in a rut, don't despair- it's Bad Hair Day, observed every year on the birthday of old time boxing promoter Don King. Just turn your head and coif.

Graffiti: **Make your dreams come true....wake up!**

Joke: The punch drunk fighter was nearly killed in a horse riding mishap. He fell from the horse and was almost trampled to death. Fortunately, the Walmart manager came out and unplugged it.

AUGUST

Today's Thought: "My wife was in labor for thirty-two hours and I was faithful to her the whole time."
-Jonathan Katz

Observance/Event: The summer is two-thirds over. Have you taken any time to goof off yet? It's Sit Back and Relax Day, a special occasion to while away a summer day. (Note: Keep this book handy in case your mate questions the validity of the holiday.)

Graffiti: **Dentists are always looking down in the mouth.**

Joke: Q: If two wrongs don't make a right, then what do two rights make?
A: An airplane

AUGUST

Today's Thought: "Talk is cheap…except when Congress does it." -Colleen Hightower

Observance/Event: It's Angel Day, an occasion to perform a random act of kindness. Our random joke in keeping with the subject is below.

Graffiti: Look out for lawyers who say they're on your side…So is appendicitis.

Joke: 100 men about to pass through the Pearly Gates were stopped by an angel. "Not so fast, guys. Before you enter Heaven, I want each of you who was henpecked during life to line up to my right and the others to my left."
99 henpecked guys lined up to the angel's right. One lone fellow stood to her left. The angel said, "How come you're standing here?" "My wife told me to."

AUGUST

Today's Thought: "I can't take a well-tanned person seriously." -Cleveland Amory

Observance/Event: Actor/comedian Jay Mohr was born on this day in 1970. And Three "Cheers" for comedic actress Shelley Long, born in 1949.

Graffiti: Mona Lisa was framed.

Joke: Fred: How is it that your company gets such great salespeople?
Red: We send our trainees out to rent an apartment and if they succeed, we give them their own territory.
Fred: So how do they prove themselves?
Red: When they knock on the landlord's door, they're carrying a tuba.

AUGUST

Today's Thought: "Ever notice that the people who are wrong seem to talk louder than anyone else?" -Andy Rooney

Observance/Event: Comedian Dave Chappelle, born in 1973, celebrates his birthday today. And it's Waffle Iron Day, commemorating the invention of the waffle iron in 1869. Prior to that, everyone's waffles were horribly wrinkled.

Graffiti: Be obscure clearly.

Joke: Donald Trump visits an old folks' home to mingle with the people and pick up a little good P.R. at the same time. He walks up to a sweet old lady in a wheelchair who smiles at him with an otherwise blank stare.
"Do you know who I am?" says The Donald.
She responds, "No, but if you ask at the desk, they'll tell you."

AUGUST

Today's Thought: "Why do men have to put the toilet seat down after using the toilet, if women don't have to put it back up when they're done." -Bob Matistic

Observance/Event: It's Kiss and Make Up Day. So kiss, make up and then bottoms up! It's also Whiskey Sour Day.

Graffiti: Never answer an anonymous letter.

Joke: After a knock-down, drag-out fight, a wife complained to her husband, "You know, I was a fool when I married you!"
He replied, "Yeah, sweetheart, but I was in love and didn't notice it."

You do not need a parachute to skydive. You only need a parachute to skydive twice.

AUGUST

26

Today's Thought: "I hope cell phones aren't bad for us, but I would like the excuse: 'I can't talk right now. You're giving me cancer.'" -Whitney Cummings

Observance/Event: Forget gun powder, pasta and astronomy. The greatest discovery ever to come out of China was introduced on this day in 580- toilet paper.

Graffiti: **Confidence is that feeling you have before you know better.**

Joke: A waiter dies suddenly and his widow is so distraught she seeks out a medium who assures her that she can speak to her husband. At the appointed time, the widow goes to a séance, presses her hands on the table and calls out, "Seymour, speak to me!" There's a terrible shriek and scary noises followed by a faint voice which cries out, "Sorry, it's not my table!"

AUGUST

27

Today's Thought: "I spent a lot of my money on booze, birds and fast cars- the rest I just squandered." -George Best

Observance/Event: It's the anniversary of the drilling of the first oil well in 1859- the first successful oil well anyway. And you know what they say: oil's well that ends well.

Graffiti: **Being a rabbit farmer is a hare-raising experience.**

Joke: Q: What's a zebra?
A: 26 times bigger than an "A" bra

You haven't experienced awkward until you try to tickle someone who isn't ticklish.

AUGUST

Today's Thought: "Personally, I'm waiting for caller IQ." -Sandra Bernhard

Observance/Event: United Parcel Service was founded in 1907. It would have been founded sooner but the Post office lost its license application in the mail.

Graffiti: How can there be self-help groups?

Joke: A 75 year-old tycoon tells his friend he's just gotten engaged to a gorgeous 21-year-old blonde. His friend says, "I know you've got a lot of money but, still in all, how could you attract a girl that young and that beautiful?"
"I told her I was 95."

AUGUST

Today's Thought: "If people don't want to come to the ballpark, how are you gonna stop them?" -Yogi Berra

Observance/Event: On this date in 1966, the Beatles played their last tour date in Candlestick Park, home of the San Francisco Giants. Ringo Starr, of course, played the drums and Willie Mays, of course, played center field.

Graffiti: Lord give me patience...and hurry!

Joke: A pirate walks into a bar with a paper towel on his head. The bartender says, "What's up with the paper towel?"
The pirate says, "Arrrrr...there's a bounty on me head!"

I tried to hang myself with a bungee chord. I kept almost dying.

AUGUST

Today's Thought: "I think the only reason you visit an Apple store is because you wonder what life is like on another planet." -Lewis Black

Observance/Event: Cantankerous comedian Lewis Black made an angry-faced entry into the world on this day in 1948.

Graffiti: **How do they get a deer to cross at those yellow road signs?**

Joke: Doctor: Henry, you've been my patient for fifty years and I have to tell you, what you are considering is dangerous. I mean a 93-year-old man marrying a 19-year-old girl. That could prove fatal. Henry: Hey Doc, the way I look at it, if she dies, she dies!

AUGUST

Today's Thought: "Did you hear the one about the lawyer who frequented only posh restaurants? He was an ambiance chaser." -Emo Phillips

Observance/Event: Comedian and actor Buddy Hackett was born in Brooklyn on this day back in 1924.

Graffiti: **The universe is expanding...why shouldn't you?**

Joke: A salesman came up to an old man rocking on his front porch when he spotted a large, fierce looking dog. "Excuse me," the salesman said, "does your dog bite?"
"Nope," the old man answered.
With that, the salesman strode up the steps, but the dog jumped at him and buried his teeth into the guy's backside.
"Hey, you said your dog didn't bite," complained the salesman.
The old man looked up and said, "He ain't my dog."

SEPTEMBER

Today's Thought: "One day my father took me aside and left me there." -Jackie Vernon

Observance/Event: Ernestine the operator, Edith Anne and all of Lily Tomlin's other characters, were born on this day in 1939.

Graffiti: Do Lipton Tea employees take coffee breaks?

Joke: Bertha: "I think this milk I bought is outdated."
Ethel: "How can you tell?"
Bertha: "Because the missing person on the carton is Jimmy Hoffa."

SEPTEMBER

Today's Thought: "Never try to impress a woman, because if you do, she'll expect you to keep up to the standard for the rest of your life." -W.C. Fields

Observance/Event: September is Be Kind to Editors and Writers month, so if you notice any errers in this book It wood be much appreciated, if you Forgive them.

Graffiti: Voodoo schools teach hex education.

Joke: A guy sees a lion approaching, falls to his knees, and prays to the Lord in hopes of being saved. All of a sudden, the lion kneels too. The guy says, "You're saying prayers too?"
"No, grace."

I don't have an attitude problem. You have a perception problem.

SEPTEMBER

Today's Thought: "Any guy who has hair on his head is overdressed." -Joe Garagiola

Observance/Event: In 1639, the first lawyer was disbarred in America. One down, two million to go.

Graffiti: George Washington didn't blame the previous administration.

Joke: Q: How many doctors does it take to change a light bulb? A: That depends on how much life insurance the light bulb has.

SEPTEMBER

Today's Thought: "I bought an ant farm. I don't know where I'm gonna find a tractor that small." -Steven Wright

Observance/Event: A reminder that this is National Chicken Month and, as such, we can't resist a "chicken crossing the road" reference... A duck was about to cross the road and the chicken said, "Don't do it, Dude. You'll never hear the end of it."

Graffiti: Gossips have a great sense of rumor.

Joke: Did you hear about the Pekingese dog that married a tomcat? Now they have a Peking Tom.

Just because nobody complains doesn't mean all parachutes are perfect.

SEPTEMBER

Today's Thought: "People who sleep like a baby usually don't have one." -Leo J. Burke

Observance/Event: The world first said "Hi Bob!" to iconic comedian Bob Newhart, born in Chicago in 1929. Also, in honor of Bob's most famous character, it's National Shrink Day.

Graffiti: **Fencing motto- In God We Thrust**

Joke: Q: Where do you find a turtle without feet?
A: Exactly where you left it.

SEPTEMBER

Today's Thought: "You might be a redneck if you're a minor drinking at your father's third wedding to your cousin." -Jeff Foxworthy

Observance/Event: Comedian/TV and radio personality Jeff Foxworthy was born today in 1958 as were alumni of two great TV comedies, *Laugh-In's* Jo Anne Worley, 1937, and *SNL's* Jane Curtin, 1947.

Graffiti: **Do pigs go through a mud-life crisis?**

Joke: An egotistical earthworm is crawling along the ground when, alongside him, he sees the most beautiful earthworm ever. "Hey, babe," the earthworm says. "Where have you been all my life?"
"Get a life, buster. I am your other end."

SEPTEMBER

Today's Thought: "Kids are like husbands. They're fine as long as they're someone else's." -Marsha Warfield

Observance/Event: The American Association for Nude Recreation got its first start in 1931 and the Miss America Pageant first gave Atlantic City a post-Labor Day boost in 1921. Bet you're thinking why didn't they just combine the two events?

Graffiti: **Lawyers wear legal briefs.**

Joke: Diner: Waiter, there's a fly in my soup!
Waiter: Don't worry, sir, he's used to the heat.

SEPTEMBER

Today's Thought: "I have just learned that penguins are monogamous for life, which doesn't really surprise me all that much, because they all look exactly alike. It's not like they're going to meet a better looking penguin someday." -Ellen DeGeneres

Observance/Event: That Cesar who ruled in the days when Comedy was King, Sid, was born this day in 1922. Also born today: Peter Sellers, 1925, and the comic strip *Blondie*, in 1930.

Graffiti: **I fixed Olivia Newton's John.**

Joke: Q: How many lawyer jokes are there?
A: None. They're all true.

No matter how much you push the envelope it will still be stationary.

SEPTEMBER

Today's Thought: "Now that I'm a parent, I understand why my father was in a bad mood a lot." -Adam Sandler

Observance/Event: Funnyman Adam Sandler was born on this date in 1966.

Graffiti: **Dating is a Hit-on-Miss proposition.**

Joke: A new bank employee was counting money very fast. The president was impressed and asked, "Where did you learn your math?"
The employee replied, "Yale."
"That's terrific. By the way, what's your name?"
"Yohnson."

SEPTEMBER

Today's Thought: "We hope that when the insects take over the world, they will remember with gratitude how we took them along on all our picnics." -Bill Vaughn

Observance/Event: It's International Make-Up Day, a day to remember someone who wronged you and bury the hatchet... hopefully in the ground!

Graffiti: **A fool and his money are soon elected.**

Joke: Doctor: Well Mr. Jones, I've completed your physical and I'd say you'll live to be ninety.
Mr. Jones: I am ninety!
Doctor: See, what'd I tell you?

Just the thought of having insomnia keeps me awake at night.

SEPTEMBER

Today's Thought: "My mom was a little weird. When I was little my mom would make chocolate frosting and she let me lick the beaters. And then she'd turn them off." -Marty Cohen

Observance/Event: It's Patriot Day.

Graffiti: It's a small world, but I wouldn't want to paint it.

Joke: A New Yorker calls his mother who lives in Florida. She answers the phone with a very weak-sounding voice.
"Mom, you don't sound good. What's wrong?"
Very feebly she answers, "I haven't eaten in 26 days."
Her son says, "26 days! How come?"
"I didn't want to be caught with food in my mouth when you called."

SEPTEMBER

Today's Thought: "I don't stop eating when I'm full. The meal isn't over when I'm full. It's over when I hate myself." -Louis C.K.

Observance/Event: Comedian Louis C.K. was born on this date in 1967.

Graffiti: Confucius say: Man who do crossword in john, have facility for words.

Joke: "I went to this Southern doctor last week."
"How could you tell he was from the South?"
He said 'Open your mouth and say ahhh will not sue'."

A bus station is where a bus stops. A train station is where a train stops. On my desk, I have a work station.

SEPTEMBER

Today's Thought: "Dogs are the leaders of the planet. If you see two life forms, one of them's making a poop, the other one's carrying it for him, who would you assume is in charge?" -Jerry Seinfeld

Observance/Event: It's International Chocolate Day, the birthday of Milton Hershey, so all you chocoholics belly up to the bar.

Graffiti: **If you can't be kind, at least be vague.**

Joke: Did you hear the one about the guy who stole the octopus from the aquarium? He was charged with eight counts of armed robbery.

SEPTEMBER

Today's Thought: "A vacation is what you take when you can no longer take what you've been taking." -Earl Wilson

Observance/Event: Not to strike a sour note but National Piano Month is almost half over.

Graffiti: **Politics makes strange bedfellows because everybody wants the same bunk!**

Joke: A dog may be man's best friend but I don't think it works the other way around. How many of your friends have you neutered?

Just read that 4,153,237 people got married last year... ummm, shouldn't that be an even number?

SEPTEMBER

15

Today's Thought: "It is generally agreed that 'Hello' is an appropriate greeting because if you entered a room and said 'Goodbye,' it could confuse a lot of people." -Dolph Sharp

Observance/Event: It's International Dot Day- a time to harness one's creativity. Comedian Steven Wright was so-inspired once that he went fishing with a dotted line. As he said, "I caught every other fish."

Graffiti: **Overweight people are those that live beyond their seams.**

Joke: Q: What do you get when you cross an elephant with a nymphomaniac?
A: A half-ton pickup.

SEPTEMBER

16

Today's Thought: "I looked up the word 'politics' in the dictionary and it's actually a combination of two words: 'poli' which means many and 'tics' which means bloodsuckers." -Jay Leno

Observance/Event: Comedic actress Amy Poehler was born in 1971 and "Smile. You're on Candid Camera" was said to Allen Funt as he was born on this date in 1914 in Brooklyn, New York.

Graffiti: **Horror movie actors can succeed beyond their wildest screams.**

Joke: A guy goes into a barbershop and asks, "What do you charge for a haircut?"
"Fourteen dollars," answers the barber. "How about for a shave?"
"That's ten bucks."
"Okay," says the guy, as he sits in the chair. "Shave my head."

SEPTEMBER

Today's Thought: "Marriage is nature's way of keeping people from fighting with strangers." -Alan King

Observance/Event: Hawkeye, Radar and Klinger began what was to be an eleven year hitch on CBS as *M*A*S*H** premiered on this date in 1972.

Graffiti: Always be sure that your end justifies your jeans.

Joke: Q: Why wouldn't the bartender serve the snake?
A: Because he couldn't hold his beer.

SEPTEMBER

Today's Thought: "Early to bed, early to rise and your girl goes out with other guys." -Bob Collins

Observance/Event: It's Chiropractic Assistants Day. It's spine time for those fine folks who, likes Kellogg's Rice Krispies, are known for their "snap, crackle and pop".

Graffiti: You can't fool all of the people all of the time. That's why there are two political parties.

Joke: A guy goes to the circus and says to the ringmaster, "I do great bird impressions."
The ringmaster says, "That's nothing special, lots of people can do great bird impressions. Scram!"
The guy says, "Okay," and flies away.

SEPTEMBER

Today's Thought: "Insanity is hereditary. You get it from your children." -Joan Rivers

Observance/Event: *Tonight Show* star Jimmy Fallon became more than just a twinkle in his parents' eyes as he was born on this date in 1974.

Graffiti: **You're only young once but you can be immature forever.**

Joke: A journeyman fighter gets knocked down. He's laying face down in the boxing ring. The ref starts to count, "One, two, three…."
The boxer's manager yells, "Don't get up until eight."
His fighter says, "No problem. What time is it now?"

SEPTEMBER

Today's Thought: "Golf, like measles, should be taught young, for, if postponed to riper years, the results may be serious." -P.G. Wodehouse

Observance/Event: It's officially National Punch Day. We'll leave the ambivalence up to your imagination (but not to our responsibility!).

Graffiti: **Hindsight is exact science.**

Joke: Mabel: Did you hear about Ethel? She had triplets and then, just a couple of weeks later, had twins!
Gertrude: Impossible! How could that happen?
Mabel: One of the twins got lost.

Do you realize that in about 40 years we'll have thousands of old ladies running around with tattoos?

SEPTEMBER

Today's Thought: "Outside of a dog, a book is man's best friend; inside of a dog, it's too dark to read." -Groucho Marx

Observance/Event: Comedic superstar Bill Murray was born this day in 1950. The *Caddyshack* golf flick actor once almost shot a 60, but the windmills kept getting in the way... And that allows us a shameless segue into the fact that it's also National Miniature Golf Day.

Graffiti: **Kleptomaniacs help themselves because they can't help themselves.**

Joke: Q: What's the opposite of irony?
A: Wrinkly

SEPTEMBER

Today's Thought: "I had the worst study habits... Then I found out what I was doing wrong. I had been highlighting with a black Magic Marker." -Jeff Altman

Observance/Event: Today is Elephant Appreciation Day... And there's nothing like appreciating a good elephant groaner- How do you know there are three elephants in your refrigerator? ... You can't close the door.

Graffiti: **The trouble with treating people like equals is pretty soon they're doing the same to you.**

Joke: Guy: Will you marry me?
Girl: No.
And they lived happily ever after.

SEPTEMBER

Today's Thought: "Did you know it's possible to
Tweet a concise, grammatical, correctly punctuated sentence
that is exactly one hundred forty characters long?" -Steve Martin
(go ahead- count 'em)

Observance/Event: *Seinfeld's* George Costanza celebrates his
birthday today. Well, not actually. Hardcore fans of the sitcom might
know that his birthday is in April, but Jason Alexander, the actor
who portrays George, was born on this day in 1959.

Graffiti: **Is there another word for synonym?**

Joke: Q: What do you call a big Irish spider?
A: Paddy Long Legs

SEPTEMBER

Today's Thought: "Movie cowboys mystify me.
How can they jump off a porch roof and onto a horse and
still sing in a normal voice?" -Bob Hope

Observance/Event: It's International Rabbit Day. Now we're
not suggesting there's going to be a celebration with all sorts of
pomp and circumstance but if you just happen to see a parade of
rabbits marching backwards, what would you call it? ...A receding
hare-line.

Graffiti: **Your lucky # is 483210568694793. Watch for
it everywhere!**

Joke: Co-workers are talking Monday morning. One says to
the other, "What did you do over the weekend?"
The other succinctly says, "Dropped hooks into the water."
The first one says, "So you went fishing, eh?"
"No, golfing."

SEPTEMBER

Today's Thought: "Mothers mold their children's minds. Some of you have done well. There are a lot of moldy-minded kids around." -Norm Crosby

Observance/Event: It's National One-Hit Wonder Day, a time to salute performers like Psy, Crazy Elephant and Eddie Cooley and the Dimples.

Graffiti: **The meek shall inherit the Earth...if that's ok with you.**

Joke: You know you're in trouble when the last thing you hear before slipping under the anesthesia is the surgeon saying, "Eenie, meenie, miney, moe...."

SEPTEMBER

Today's Thought: "Nobody goes to that restaurant anymore. It's too crowded." -Yogi Berra

Observance/Event: Shamu, Sea World's whale of a star, was born on this date in 1985. They call the folks in charge of his party "orcanizers."

Graffiti: **Four out of five doctors recommend another doctor.**

Joke: As a women's lib zealot boarded a crowded bus, one man got to his feet.
"No, you must not give up your seat. I insist," she said.
"You can insist all you like, lady," replied the man. "This is my stop."

SEPTEMBER

Today's Thought: "I used to be a heavy gambler. But now I just make mental bets. That's how I lost my mind."
-Steve Allen

Observance/Event: *The Tonight Show*, with Steve Allen as its original host, made it debut on NBC-TV on this date in 1954.

Graffiti: A backseat driver never runs out of gas.

Joke: Frick: My uncle just went to court on that liquor store robbery charge.
Frack: How'd he do?
Frick: He took the fifth.

SEPTEMBER

Today's Thought: "If you want to know how your girl will treat you after marriage, just listen to her talk to her little brother." -Sam Levenson

Observance/Event: It's National Good Neighbor Day so wait until tomorrow before you start raking those leaves into your neighbor's yard.

Graffiti: Wall Street is the capital of capital.

Joke: Then there was the Indian chief named Running Water. He had two daughters, Hot and Cold, and a son named Luke.

To the man on crutches, dressed in camouflage, who stole my wallet- you can hide, but you can't run.

SEPTEMBER

Today's Thought: "Hospitals are weird. They put you in a private room and then give you a public gown." -Milton Berle

Observance/Event: This week, the week immediately preceding Fire Prevention Week, is Chimney Sweep Week, otherwise known as "flue season."

Graffiti: **Just because love is blind it doesn't mean that you can feel your way around.**

Joke: Did you hear about the dog that requires three baths a day? It's called a Shampoodle.

SEPTEMBER

Today's Thought: "Never lend your car to anyone whom you've given birth." -Erma Bombeck

Observance/Event: Everybody's favorite modern stone-age family, The Flintstones, first rocked the airwaves on this date in 1960.

Graffiti: **The biggest cause of divorce is marriage.**

Joke: A man takes his pooch to a dog psychiatrist and says, "Every time my dog hears a bell ring, he goes into the corner." "That's perfectly normal," replies the shrink. "He's a Boxer."

Why do you need a driver's license to buy liquor when you can't drink and drive?

OCTOBER

Today's Thought: "The amount of sleep required by the average person is about five minutes more." -Max Kauffmann

Observance/Event: October 1st, 1920, gave us the Walter Matthau half of the Odd Couple while the same day in 1950 gave us the Randy half of the Quaid brothers.

Graffiti: **Donald Duck is not goofy, but he's still a quack.**

Joke: Q: What do cryogenicists sing when interring a new body? A: "Freeze a jolly good fellow!"

OCTOBER

Today's Thought: "Marriage is a wonderful institution, but who wants to live in an institution?" -Groucho Marx

Observance/Event: October is National Sarcastics Awareness Month- yeah, like we should have told you yesterday so you'd have that whole extra day to celebrate. I mean its sooo important...

Graffiti: **Pediatricians are men of little patients.**

Joke: Did you hear the one about the guy who only told jokes in the bathroom? He was the life of the potty!

OCTOBER

Today's Thought: "The secret into staying young is to live honestly, eat slowly and lie about your age." -Lucille Ball

Observance/Event: Sandwiched between the first and second weekends of October is National Pickled Pepper Week. This year, as a nod to the metric system, Peter Piper will pick 8.8 liters of pickled peppers.

Graffiti: **A closed mouth catches no flies.**

Joke: Q: What kind of survey did Betsy Ross take to determine what the new U.S. banner should look like?
A: A flag poll

OCTOBER

Today's Thought: "Opera is when a guy gets stabbed in the back and, instead of bleeding, he sings." -Ed Gardner

Observance/Event: October is both National Pizza Month and National Pasta Month, encouraging you to gorge on these high-calorie delicacies. Hope November is "National Liposuction Month".

Graffiti: **They call it Middle Age because that's where it shows first.**

Joke: A guy goes into an animal auction and bids on a parrot. Every time he makes a bid, there's another bid to top him. Finally, he wins. He goes over to the parrot and says, "Do you talk?"
The parrot says,"Who do you think has been bidding against you?"

OCTOBER

Today's Thought: "The biggest seller is cookbooks and the second best are diet books- how to eat what you just learned how to cook." -Andy Rooney

Observance/Event: It's World Teachers' Day- an occasion this joke book publisher can really appreciate. He spent three of his favorite years in the fourth grade.

Graffiti: **I've never had premonitions, but I think one day I might.**

Joke: Then there was the dentist who complimented the hockey player on his nice, even teeth: one, three, five, seven and nine were missing.

OCTOBER

Today's Thought: "The secret of managing is to keep the guys who hate you away from the guys who are undecided." -Casey Stengel

Observance/Event: The first full week of October is…let's see, I had that around here somewhere…oh yeah, over here. Nope, that's not it…in the drawer maybe, no…oh, here- under the coffee mug… it's Get Organized Week.

Graffiti: **Eve gave Adam quite a ribbing.**

Joke: The wife sees her hubbie lounging on the couch and says,"When are you thinking of cleaning out the garage?" He replies, "In a little while, dear. Right now I'm thinking of mowing the lawn."

OCTOBER

Today's Thought: "My kitchen floor is sticky and I had to do something about it. So finally I went out and bought some slippers." -Sarah Silverman

Observance/Event: This observance may have a ring to it. On this date in 1828, the bathtub was introduced to the world.

Graffiti: **No sense being pessimistic. It wouldn't work anyway.**

Joke: Q: Where does a tennis player go for entertainment?
A: Volley-wood

OCTOBER

Today's Thought: "I majored in nursing but I had to drop it because I ran out of milk." -Judy Tenuta

Observance/Event: It's Take A Fall Day, in honor of Chevy Chase who stumbled his way to fame and fortune and who was born on this day in 1943.

Graffiti: **Lazy people do diddly-squats.**

Joke: Q: What's the difference between a lawyer and a vulture?
A: Lawyers can take off their wingtips.

God gave us the brain to work out problems. However, we use it to create more problems.

OCTOBER

Today's Thought: "Lot of strip clubs in Florida... good grief...Florida has so many strip clubs, they need to change their state flag to a brass pole." -Wanda Sykes

Observance/Event: October is Auto Battery Safety Month so if you want to get a jump on things and really get a charge out of the occasion, you need a positive attitude, especially if you're run down.

Graffiti: **You can't be late until you show up.**

Joke: Q: How do you keep a simpleton in suspense?
A:

OCTOBER

Today's Thought: "There are so many TV commercials now that what used to be a simple station break, sounds like a compound fracture." -Monta Crane

Observance/Event: Get your just desserts on National Dessert Day, the second Thursday in October, an observance that takes the cake.

Graffiti: **Save face...don't lose your head!**

Joke: A guy runs into a bar and yells, "Quick. Do you know a cure for a terrible case of hiccups?"
Without saying a word, the bartender gives the guy a swift kick to the stomach, forcing him to gasp for air.
"I bet you don't have the hiccups now," says the bartender.
"No, but my wife who's in the car does."

OCTOBER

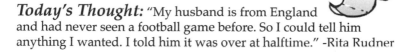

Today's Thought: "My husband is from England and had never seen a football game before. So I could tell him anything I wanted. I told him it was over at halftime." -Rita Rudner

Observance/Event: It's the birthday of Henry Ford and Kiss Your Car Day. You might want to run it through the car wash first.

Graffiti: **The wages of sin are usually unreported.**

Joke: Did you hear the one about the flight school that went out of business? All they offered were crash courses.

OCTOBER

Today's Thought: "She's the kind of woman who climbed the ladder of success...wrong by wrong." -Mae West

Observance/Event: It's International Moment of Frustration Scream Day. Instead of moanin' and groanin' all year long, save it all up for one cathartic psyche-cleansing moment of primal scream release.

Graffiti: **Headaches are all in your mind!**

Joke: And then there was the woman with what they call an "Indiana Figure"...a large South Bend.

Never get into fights with ugly people. They have nothing to lose.

OCTOBER

13

Today's Thought: "I used to think that the human brain was the most fascinating part of the body. Then I realized, well, look what's telling me that." -Emo Philips

Observance/Event: The second week in October is National Pet Peeve Week, a time to vent your frustration with the thing that annoys you the most...like all these silly observances.

Graffiti: **People who think they know it all really annoy those of us who do.**

Joke: Prosecutor: Why did you shoot your husband with a bow and arrow?
Defendant: I didn't want to wake the children.

OCTOBER

14

Today's Thought: "As a child my family's menu consisted of two choices. Take it or leave it." -Buddy Hackett

Observance/Event: It's Be Bald and Be Free Day, a day for the hairing-impaired everywhere to buff up the old chrome dome and wear it with pride.

Graffiti: **There are more important things in life than money but none of them will go out with you if you're broke.**

Joke: Did you hear about the woman driver who went to heaven? She drove through the Pearly Gates and took one of them with her.

"I'm sorry" and "I apologize" mean the same thing- except when you're at a funeral.

OCTOBER

Today's Thought: "No matter how bad things get you got to go on living, even if it kills you." -Sholom Aleichem

Observance/Event: Grumble and grouse away, it's National Grouch Day...a hearty "Bah, humbug!" to all.

Graffiti: **You're not fat- you're just easier to see.**

Joke: Two dogs are walking together on the side of the street. Suddenly, one dog says, "Just a second. I'll be right back." He walks over to the other side of the street and sniffs all around a fire hydrant. Then he comes back.
"What was that for?" asks his doggy pal.
"Oh, I was just checking my messages."

OCTOBER

Today's Thought: "It's all right to hold a conversation, but you should let go of it now and then." -Richard Armour

Observance/Event: It's Dictionary Day. We'll take that as a day to have fun with words- as in pun-ishment. Here goes: What did the DNA say to the other DNA?... "Do these genes make me look fat?"

Graffiti: **Wine is grape expectations.**

Joke: Then there was the judge who kept a mirror on the wall of his chambers. Whenever he passed it, he'd ask, "Who's the fairest of them all?"

Knowledge is knowing a tomato is a fruit. Wisdom is not putting it in a fruit salad.

OCTOBER

Today's Thought: "The two biggest websites right now are Wikipedia, where you go to learn about things you care about, and Facebook, where you go to learn about people you stopped caring about years ago." -Craig Ferguson

Observance/Event: George Wendt of *Cheers* fame got his first applause on the bottom as was the "Norm" on this day in 1948.

Graffiti: **It's better to beat a dead horse than a live one.**

Joke: Then there were the two very competitive silkworms who raced each other. It ended in a tie.

OCTOBER

Today's Thought: "I have opinions of my own - strong opinions- but I don't always agree with them." -President George W. Bush

Observance/Event: Sitcom actress Erin Moran (Joannie on *Happy Days*) was born on this day in beautiful downtown Burbank, in 1961.

Graffiti: **Health food is sickening.**

Joke: A fellow came home from a round of golf and was greeted at the door by his wife dressed in some very alluring attire.
"Tie me up," she cooed, "and do anything you want."
So he tied her up and played another round.

Somewhere an old lady reads a book on how to use the Internet, while a young boy googles "how to read a book".

OCTOBER

Today's Thought: "I get my exercise running to the funerals of my friends who exercise." -Barry Gray

Observance/Event: The Wellness Permission League says it's Evaluate Your Life Day. With or without permission of said league, we're going to evaluate your life for you: You are a nobody. Nobody's perfect. Therefore, you are perfect!

Graffiti: **Can you daydream at night?**

Joke: Q: Why did the racehorse hide behind the tree?
A: He wanted to change his jockeys.

OCTOBER

Today's Thought: "Should not the Society of Indexers be known as 'Indexers, Society of, The'?" -Keith Waterhouse

Observance/Event: Clowning around took center stage on this date in 1873 when P.T. Barnum's "Greatest Show on Earth" opened the first hippodrome in New York City.

Graffiti: **If life gives you melons, you're probably dyslexic.**

Joke: Two cannibals are eating a clown when one says to the other, "Does this taste funny to you?"

Why does someone believe you when you say there are four billion stars, but check when you say the paint is wet?

OCTOBER

Today's Thought: "I found out why cats drink out of the toilet. My mother me it's because it's cold in there. And I'm like, 'How did my mother know that?'" -Wendy Liebman

Observance/Event: The third week in October is National Shampoo Week, the one time each year you are encouraged to work yourself into a lather.

Graffiti: How come it isn't spelled "bureaucrazy"?

Joke: A guy with two left feet walks into a shoe store and says, "Got any flip-flips?"

OCTOBER

Today's Thought: "To paraphrase Shakespeare, it's better to have loved and lost than to stay home every night and download increasingly shameful pornography." -Rajesh Koothrappali, *The Big Bang Theory*

Observance/Event: Reverend Jim Ignatowski's alter-ego, Christopher Lloyd (*Taxi, Back to the Future*) was born in Stamford, Connecticut, on this day in 1938.

Graffiti: Stop by for a spell. (Seen in Salem, MA)

Joke: Maybe you've heard that alimony is simply a contraction of "all his money".

I hate when I am about to hug someone really sexy and my face hits the mirror.

OCTOBER

Today's Thought: "A conference is a gathering of important people who singly can do nothing but together can decide that nothing can be done." -Fred Allen

Observance/Event: "Heeeeerreee's Johnny!" was heard for the first time on this date in 1925 as the future "King of Late Night", Johnny Carson was born.

Graffiti: **Doctor Jekyll had something to Hyde.**

Joke: "You must be the worst caddie in the world," said the dejected golfer after a horrible day out on the links. "I doubt it, sir," replied the caddie. "That would be too much of a coincidence."

OCTOBER

Today's Thought: "If there is a God, give me a sign!...See, I told you that the klamaf slinfirrt gupttoorrupt..." -Steve Martin

Observance/Event: Alonzo Phillips struck it rich as he patented matches in 1836. Here's one guy who really set the world on fire.

Graffiti: **Happiness is having a clear conscience or none at all.**

Joke: A vacationer visiting Africa sees an old witch doctor lying in the road with his ear to the ground. He gets a little closer to hear the witch doctor mumbling, "Man in van, come by a half hour ago." "Wow! You can tell that by listening to the ground?" "No. He run over me."

OCTOBER

Today's Thought: "The average, healthy, well-adjusted adult gets up at seven-thirty in the morning feeling just plain terrible." -Jean Kerr

Observance/Event: It's Sourest Day. Honor all of those sourpusses out there today. You know, the ones who look as if they were weaned on a pickle.

Graffiti: **Politicians are blame droppers.**

Joke: Q: Why is consumer advocate Ralph Nader humorless?
A: Because you can't recall a joke.

OCTOBER

Today's Thought: "The airline people are always telling you that it's safer to fly than drive. Why don't they tell you the other statistic…that it's safer to crash in a car than in a plane?" -Brad Stein

Observance/Event: Garry Trudeau's *Doonesbury* cartoon kicked off on this day in 1970.

Graffiti: **Is there a time limit on fortune cookie predictions?**

Joke: Q: What's the only thing that can get more money out of you than the IRS?
A: The MRS

She wanted a puppy. But I didn't want a puppy. So we compromised. We got a puppy.

OCTOBER

Today's Thought: "If you talk to God, you're religious. If God talks to you, you're psychotic." -Dr. House, *House*

Observance/Event: On this date in 1939, *Monty Python's* John Cleese made his first "entrance" in Weston-Super-Mare, England.

Graffiti: **Support the right to arm bears.**

Joke: Diner: "Waiter, why isn't there any soup on the menu?" Waiter: "I wiped it off."

OCTOBER

Today's Thought: "Never brag about your ancestors coming over on the Mayflower. The immigration laws weren't as strict in those days." -Lew Lehr

Observance/Event: The first baby born in flight happened high above Miami, Florida, on this date in 1929. Wonder if they charged the mother for another ticket?

Graffiti: **Instant gratification takes much too long.**

Joke: Upon inspecting the hunter's credentials, the game warden said, "This is last year's license."
"I know," said the hunter. "I'm only shooting at the deer I missed last year."

You're not fat. You're just easier to see.

OCTOBER

Today's Thought: "I started out with nothing. I still have most of it." -Michael Davis

Observance/Event: It's Internet Day, honoring the 1969 origin of the first remote connection between two computers. In keeping with the day, we offer you this groaner: How do trees get on the Internet? They log in.

Graffiti: **A cardboard belt is a waist of paper.**

Joke: Q: How does Donald Trump screw in a light bulb?
A: He holds it up in the air and the whole world revolves around him.

OCTOBER

Today's Thought: "I haven't spoken to my wife in years. I did not want to interrupt her." -Henny Youngman

Observance/Event: This was a "cool" day in 1945 as Henry Winkler (the Fonz on *Happy Days*) was born in New York City.

Graffiti: **Old limbo dancers never die, they just go under.**

Joke: The day Ralph retired from the Post Office, his supervisor gathered everyone together and made a little speech ending with, "Ralph, after thirty-years in the United States Post Office, what have you learned?"
Ralph replied, "Don't mail my gold watch. I'll take it with me."

Regular naps prevent old age- especially if you take them while driving.

OCTOBER

Today's Thought: "I went to a Halloween party dressed as the equator. As people walked towards me they got warmer." -Steven Wright

Observance/Event: The world got a very special sweet for Halloween on this date in 1950…comedic actor John Candy.

Graffiti: Philosophy of a skunk: I stink, therefore I am.

Joke: Q. What do you get when you cross a pumpkin with a basketball great?
A. A Shaq-o'-lantern

NOVEMBER

Today's Thought: "The right to bear arms goes back to our Constitution. I feel that way because man is by nature a hunter, and also because a moose doesn't vote." -Johnny Carson

Observance/Event: It's National Author's Day so, in honor of the occasion, our publishers have allowed us to tell you this one- Did you hear about the incompetent editor who became a joke book publisher? He was "moved upstairs" after using white-out on the computer screen.

Graffiti: Is the "S" or the "C" silent in the word "scent"?

Joke: Frick: My brother ran the governor's re-election campaign hoping to get a state job.
Frack: What's he doing now?
Frick: Nothing. He got the job.

NOVEMBER

Today's Thought: "The insurance man told me that the accident policy covered falling off the roof but not hitting the ground." -Tommy Cooper

Observance/Event: Down in Dog Patch and now in many other far-flung locales, the first Saturday in November is Sadie Hawkins Day, a chance for the ladies to pester men for dates. Conversely, it's also a chance for men to claim that they're washing their hair or doing their nails that night.

Graffiti: **There are 3 types of people in this world-ones who can count, and ones who can't.**

Joke: Q: Do you know the most tech-savvy Israeli Prime Minister?
A: Netandyahoo

NOVEMBER

Today's Thought: I'd rather have thieves than neighbors. The thieves don't impose. They just want your things. Neighbors want your time. -Larry David, *Curb Your Enthusiasm*

Observance/Event: Funnylady Roseanne Barr was born on this day in 1952 and humorist Dennis Miller followed a year later... A reminder for all you arachibutyrophobiacs (Look that up in your Funk & Wagnall's!): It's Peanut Butter Lover's Month.

Graffiti: **He who throws mud loses ground.**

Joke: Q: What do politicians and criminals have in common?
A: They take the money and run.

A recent study has found that women who carry a little extra weight live longer than the men who mention it.

NOVEMBER

Today's Thought: "Identical twins. I'm glad they're identical 'cause you save money on photographs. That's what I like. Yeah. Here's my little boy. I got another one just like it."
-Ray Romano

Observance/Event: The loveable "Naughton", Art Carney (*The Honeymooners*), was born in 1918. Also born on this date in 1960 was comedian/actress/TV host Kathy Griffin.

Graffiti: **Male deer have buck teeth.**

Joke: Q: What do you call a man with a receipt on his head?
A: Bill

NOVEMBER

Today's Thought: "The reason God made man before woman was because he didn't want any suggestions."
-Sam Levenson

Observance/Event: November is National Football Widows Month, an observance to recognize the sacrifices of sports-spurned spouses during this, the fall and winter of their discontent.

Graffiti: **When the going gets tough, the tough gets prune juice.**

Joke: "How do you do well with the women?"
"The most important thing in wooing a girl is a romantic setting."
"Give me an example of a romantic setting."
"Any setting that has a diamond in it."

NOVEMBER

Today's Thought: "What I need is a search engine that, no matter what I type in, comes back with GO BACK TO WORK." -Dave Barry

Observance/Event: The Flying Nun, Sally Field, was born on this date in 1946 in Pasadena, California. And that reminds us... What do you call Sister Superior when she gets to heaven? Nun of the above.

Graffiti: Two wrongs don't make a right, but three lefts will.

Joke: Diner: Waiter, there's a footprint in my breakfast!
Waiter: Well, sir, you ordered an omelet and told me to step on it.

NOVEMBER

Today's Thought: "When you are in love with someone, you want to be near him all the time, except when you are out buying things and charging them to him." -Miss Piggy

Observance/Event: On this day in 1874, cartoonist Thomas Nast created the Republican elephant to symbolize the G.O.P. Word has it that the elephant was so excited that it broke out in hives and had to go to the pachydermatologist.

Graffiti: Woodworkers have more vices.

Joke: Q: Why couldn't they play cards on Noah's ark?
A: Because the elephant sat on the deck.

My Internet is so slow, it's faster to drive to the Google headquarters and just ask them stuff in person.

NOVEMBER

Today's Thought: "I ask people why they have deer heads on their walls. They always say because it's such a beautiful animal. I think my mother is attractive, but I have photographs of her." -Ellen DeGeneres

Observance/Event: Believe it or not, it's Aid and Abet Punsters Day. It's a day to laugh instead of groan at incredibly dreadful puns. The folks who founded this day claim that this is the all-time greatest triple pun: "Though he's not very humble, there's no police like Holmes."

Graffiti: **Rehab is for quitters.**

Joke: Frog: "Hey waiter! There's no fly in my soup!"

NOVEMBER

Today's Thought: "I have no self-confidence. When girls tell me yes, I tell them to think it over." -Rodney Dangerfield

Observance/Event: Some people say November is International Drum Month. Others say it's in May. We've decided to march to the beat of a different drum and have created our own celebration: Today is Rimshot Day. See our contribution below.

Graffiti: **If you choke a Smurf, what color does it turn?**

Joke: Two cowboys are riding along out West when they hear the ominous sound of drums. One of the cowboys says, "I don't like the sound of those drums."
Off in the distance, they hear an Indian yell, "He's not our regular drummer!" (ba-dum-bum-CHING!)

NOVEMBER

Today's Thought: "My heroes are Larry Bird, Admiral Byrd, Lady Bird, Sheryl Crow, Chick Corea, the inventor of bird seed, and anyone who reads to you even if she's tired." -Big Bird

Observance/Event: They're throwing a big bash over at 123 Sesame Street today in honor of the TV show's premiere on this date in 1969...This exchange between Bert and Ernie was overheard at the festivities- "Would you like some ice cream, Ernie?" ..."Sherbert."

Graffiti: **Laugh and the world laughs with you... snore and you sleep alone.**

Joke: Did you hear the one about the surgeon who moonlighted as a comedian? He always had everybody in stitches.

NOVEMBER

Today's Thought: "Ninety percent of the game (baseball) is half mental." -Yogi Berra

Observance/Event: Madcap Jonathan Winters improvised his first baby impression on this day in 1925.

Graffiti: **Talk is cheap...As long as it isn't lawyers who are doing the talking.**

Joke: A deer, a skunk and a duck walk into a bar. They each ask for a beer. The bartender says, "That'll be three dollars."
The deer says, "I don't have a buck."
The skunk says, "I don't have a scent."
The duck says, "Put it on my bill."

NOVEMBER

Today's Thought: "Croutons are kept in a 'Stay-Fresh' pouch. How nice. Croutons are stale bread. If we left these open all night they could only get better. Nobody has ever gone back to the store and said, 'I need my money back. These are going fresh'." -Steve Bruner

Observance/Event: In 1745, a pub in Ireland hosted the world's first Happy Hour.

Graffiti: **He who laughs last, thinks slowest.**

Joke: A camel walks into a bar with a mummy on its back. The mummy gets off the camel, sits on a bar stool and the bartender says, "Can I get you a drink?"
The mummy says, "No, I just came here to unwind."

NOVEMBER

Today's Thought: "There's a great woman behind every idiot." -John Lennon

Observance/Event: Caryn Elaine Johnson was born on this day in 1955. You know her better as comedian/actress/TV personality Whoopi Goldberg. And yes, the first part of her stage name was taken from a whoopee cushion…Also born on this date, in 1967, is TV host Jimmy Kimmel.

Graffiti: **What hair color do they put on the driver's licenses of bald men?**

Joke: Two hillbillies are hunting when they come across some tracks in the woods.
"Look! Deer tracks," says the first hillbilly.
"Naah, those are moose tracks. I know moose tracks when I see 'em," says the second hillbilly.
A few moments later they got run over by a train.

NOVEMBER

Today's Thought: "If I get married again, I want a guy there with a drum to do rimshots during the vows."
-Sam Kinison

Observance/Event: It's National Pickle Day and we have a dilly for you. Why shouldn't you shoot pool using a pickle?... Because you'll find the cue cumbersome.

Graffiti: Repeal the banana!

Joke: A guy goes to a doctor with a duck on his head. The doctor says, "What can I do for you?"
"I'd like this wart on my foot removed," replies the duck.

NOVEMBER

Today's Thought: "The best way to get most husbands to do something is to suggest that perhaps they're too old to do it." -Shirley MacLaine

Observance/Event: It's National Philanthropy Day. Speaking of which... An IRS agent calls Father Murphy and says, "Can you help us?" "I can." "Do you know a Herb Klotz?" "I do." "Does he belong to your parish?" "He does." "Did he donate $10,000 to the church?" "He will!"

Graffiti: Truth is stranger than fiction but not nearly as popular.

Joke: Then there was the horse that came in so late the jockey was wearing pajamas.

NOVEMBER

Today's Thought: "Everyone is on this low-fat craze now. The Mayo Clinic just changed its name to the Balsam Vinaigrette Clinic." -Buzz Nutley

Observance/Event: Today is Fast Food Day…And now this Whopper of a groaner: A Big Mac walks into a saloon. The bartender says, "Sorry, we don't serve food here."

Graffiti: **A female moth is a myth.**

Joke: Then there was the dog that saw a sign, "WET PAINT." He did.

NOVEMBER

Today's Thought: "A new study found that nearly one out of three people can't resist using Facebook while in the bathroom. I'm just grateful they're not using Skype." -Conan O'Brien

Observance/Event: *Taxi's* Danny DeVito was born on this date in 1944.

Graffiti: **If you've lost your memory, forget about it.**

Joke: On the street corner in New York a vendor waved a bouquet at a passerby. "Take home a bundle for your wife, sir."
The passerby replied, "I'm not married."
"Then take a bundle for your sweetheart."
"I don't have a girlfriend, either."
"Well, then, take home a couple of bundles to celebrate."

NOVEMBER

Today's Thought: "'Politically correct' is a contradiction in terms." -Sparky Anderson Kreismer

Observance/Event: Today is the birthday of The Big Cheese himself- Mickey Mouse, debuted in *Steamboat Willie* in 1928.

Graffiti: **99% of lawyers give the rest a bad name.**

Joke: St. Peter answers the door to the Pearly Gates and sees a man standing there. As he's about to welcome him to Heaven, suddenly the guy disappears. A little while later there's another knock. It's the same guy. St. Peter opens the door and the guy vanishes again. Minutes go by and there's another knock. This time, St. Peter opens the door quickly and blurts out, "Hey, are you playing games with me?"
"No," the guy replies anxiously. "They're trying to resuscitate me."

NOVEMBER

Today's Thought: "In Russia we only had two TV channels. Channel One was propaganda. Channel Two consisted of a KGB officer telling you, 'Turn back at once to Channel One!'" -Yakov Smirnoff

Observance/Event: Irked by all those smiley face emojis? Well, get out there and wish everyone ill on Have a Bad Day Day. Here's hoping it's totally lousy.

Graffiti: **People in cloisters shouldn't eat oysters!**

Joke: Two cannibal women are talking. One says, "I don't know what to make of my husband."
The other one says, "Get a recipe book."

My resume is just a list of things I hope you never ask me to do.

NOVEMBER

Today's Thought: "I bought a tube of Krazy Glue and the label fell off." -Jay Leno

Observance/Event: Their mother's favorite Smothers Brother, Dick, was born on this date in 1938.

Graffiti: **Beauty is in the eyes of the beer holder.**

Joke: The minister droned on and on but before finally wrapping up, he apologized to the congregation for the large Band-Aid on his face.
"I was so busy thinking about my sermon as I was shaving that I cut my face."
From the back came a voice, "Next time, think about shaving and cut the sermon."

NOVEMBER

Today's Thought: "I used to work at McDonald's making minimum wage. You know what that means when someone pays you minimum wage? You know what your boss was trying to say? It's like, 'Hey, if I could pay you less, I would, but it's against the law.'" -Chris Rock

Observance/Event: That Girl, Marlo Thomas, was born in 1938 and one of those *Laugh-In* girls, Goldie Hawn, came along in 1945.

Graffiti: **The past was much like the present, only longer.**

Joke: A king was fanatical about hunting and spent virtually all of his time doing so. Finally, the people in his kingdom became fed up with his pastime and overthrew him. In all of history, this is the only known example of reign being cancelled on account of game.

NOVEMBER

Today's Thought: "I'll never forget my youth. I was teacher's pet. She couldn't afford a dog." -Rodney Dangerfield

Observance/Event: Rodney Dangerfield began a life of no respect on this day in 1921.

Graffiti: **Shake a family tree and you're bound to get a few nuts.**

Joke: Returning from a movie intermission, a man asked the person on the aisle, "Pardon me, but did I step on your feet on the way out?"
"You certainly did," was the curt reply.
"C'mon, Honey," the man called to his wife, "this is the right row."

NOVEMBER

Today's Thought: "You know what blows my mind? Women can see breasts any time they want. You just look down, and there they are. How you get any work done is beyond me." -Joey Tribbiani, *Friends*

Observance/Event: Harpo Marx joined the act this day in 1893.

Graffiti: **Would a fly without wings be called a walk?**

Joke: A guy prays to the Lord to win the lottery, promising to do good deeds when he does. This goes on for weeks, but he never wins. Finally he says, "God, I don't understand. I'm a good person. I've been praying for a long time to win the lottery. How come I haven't?"
A thundering voice from the heavens responds, "You gotta buy a ticket!"

NOVEMBER

Today's Thought: "Guys are lucky because they get to grow mustaches. I wish I could. It's like having a little pet for your face." -Anita Wise

Observance/Event: The Big Yin, Scottish comic Billy Connolly, was born on this date in 1942.

Graffiti: **What's the speed of dark?**

Joke: Little Johnny's sitting by the river, fishing with his grandpa. While waiting for the fish to bite, Grandpa decides to teach him a lesson. He pours a flask of whiskey into a glass. Then he reaches for the bait, pulls out a couple of worms and puts them in the glass full of liquor. The worms become lifeless almost immediately. "Look here, Johnny, those worms have died. What does that tell you?" "Simple, Grandpa. Drink whiskey and you won't get worms."

NOVEMBER

Today's Thought: "Have you ever noticed that people who live in mobile home parks never ever move? I mean, look folks, if you're going to live in the same place for fifty years, get rid of the wheels." -Shashi Bhatia

Observance/Event: Comedic actor John Larroquette (*The John Larroquette Show, Night Court*) got his start this day in 1947.

Graffiti: **Say what you want about deaf people...**

Joke: Q: What did the turkey say to the turkey hunter?
A: "Quack, quack, quack!"

You have the capacity to learn from your mistakes, and you will learn a lot today.

NOVEMBER

Today's Thought: "Every man sees in his relatives a series of grotesque caricatures of himself." -H.L. Mencken

Observance/Event: Master mimic Rich Little kicked up the population of Ottawa, Canada, by one today in 1938.

Graffiti: **Eat, drink and be fat and drunk.**

Joke: Car dealer: I've got bad news and worse news.
Customer: Give me the bad news first.
Car dealer: Your car won't start.
Customer: What's the worse news?
Car dealer: The payments won't stop.

NOVEMBER

Today's Thought: "I asked a bartender for a double. He brought me out a guy who looks just like me."
-Rodney Dangerfield

Observance/Event: The first Macy's Thanksgiving Day parade took place in New York City on this date in 1924. Ah, Thanksgiving. According to Jay Leno, it's when the Indians said, "Well, this has been fun, but we know you have a long voyage back to England."

Graffiti: **Keep the dream alive. Hit the snooze button.**

Joke: A psychiatrist says to his patient, "Why don't you start at the beginning?"
"Alright, in the beginning I created the heavens and the Earth…"

Everybody repeat after me: "We are all individuals."

NOVEMBER

Today's Thought: "I've been on so many blind dates, I should get a free dog." -Wendy Liebman

Observance/Event: Comedian, writer and former talk show host Jon Stewart made his first daily show on this date in 1962.

Graffiti: **Too many birthdays can kill you.**

Joke: Three old geezers were sitting on a park bench. The one in the middle was reading a newspaper while the other two were pretending to fish. A policeman on the beat watched as they baited imaginary hooks, cast their lines and reeled in their fake catches. "Do you know these two?" the cop asked the guy reading the paper. "Sure. They're buddies of mine."
"Well, they're disturbing everyone. You better get them outta here!"
"Yes, officer," said the guy, and with that he furiously began rowing.

NOVEMBER

Today's Thought: "I'm a huge fan of mine. I go to just about every show I do." -Howie Mandel

Observance/Event: Howie Mandel took the deal and was born on this date in 1955.

Graffiti: **Do rivers sleep in river beds?**

Joke: "So Al, I never asked you. How come you had fourteen kids?"
"Well, Pete, my wife always took her hearing aid off before bedtime and as we turned in I always asked her, 'So…you want to go to sleep or what?' And she'd always say, 'What?'"

Well, here I am! What are your other two wishes?

NOVEMBER

Today's Thought: "Why do they call it the restroom? Is there anybody resting in this room?" -Dane Cook

Observance/Event: It's Stay Home Because You're Well Day. What fun is it staying home when you're sick? Call in well and enjoy your robust good health. (Please note that *The Bathroom Joke Almanac* is not responsible for any adverse effect on your career should you chose to observe this holiday.)

Graffiti: **Ancestry is hereditary.**

Joke: A golf club walks into a bar. The bartender says, "Sorry, I can't serve you."
The golf club says, "Why?"
"Because you're going to be driving."

DECEMBER

Today's Thought: "I think crime pays. The hours are good. You travel a lot." -Woody Allen

Observance/Event: Woody Allen began accumulating neuroses this day in 1935 and Comedy Central's #1 all-time comedian, Richard Pryor, came along in 1940.

Graffiti: **Show me a man who's afraid of Christmas and I'll show you a Noel Coward.**

Joke: Q: Why are the colors of Christmas green and red?
A: Because you spend all of your green and wind up in the red.

Living on Earth is expensive, but it does include a free trip around the sun.

DECEMBER

Today's Thought: "When I was a kid in Houston, we were so poor we couldn't afford the last two letters, so we called ourselves po'."-George Foreman

Observance/Event: On this date in 1933, Bertil Clason and Sigrid Carlson were wed in the first transatlantic telephone wedding. (Talk about "phoning it in"!)

Graffiti: **I used to hear voices, but we're fine now.**

Joke: Q: How many Cleveland Browns does it take to screw in a light bulb?
A: One, and the other ten to recover the fumble.

DECEMBER

Today's Thought: "Every room is a bathroom when you're wearing Depends." -Jimmy Fallon

Observance/Event: It's Bake a Biscuit Day, celebrated on the birthday of Charles Pillsbury. Since the holidays are almost upon us, feel free to substitute cookies.

Graffiti: **Throwing acid is wrong, in some people's eyes.**

Joke: Shirley came home to find a card taped to her door that read, "Merry Christmas from the custodial staff."
"How nice," she thought. A week later she again found a card taped to her door. It read, "Merry Christmas from the custodial staff-Second Notice."

DECEMBER

Today's Thought: "My grandfather's been senile all his life but nobody ever told me and I've been taking all his advice." -Steve Sweeny

Observance/Event: It's Cookie Day, a day to take heed to the words of Cookie Monster: "C is for cookie, that's good enough for me!"

Graffiti: **Where do they get the seeds to plant seedless watermelons?**

Joke: Diner: Waiter! Your thumb is in my soup!
Waiter: Don't worry sir. It isn't hot.

DECEMBER

Today's Thought: "Scientists announced today that they have found a cure for apathy. However, they claim no one has shown the slightest bit of interest in it." -George Carlin

Observance/Event: Today marks Bathtub Party Day, a time to immerse yourself in a long, hot bath. (Better yet, save water; bathe with a friend.)

Graffiti: **One day you're the best thing since sliced bread. The next, you're toast.**

Joke: Frick: I'm in big trouble with my girlfriend. She showed the engagement ring I gave her to the girls at work.
Frack: Didn't they admire it?
Frick: Admire it? Half of them recognized it.

DECEMBER

Today's Thought: "I was walking down the street wearing glasses when the prescription ran out." -Steven Wright

Observance/Event: Steven Wright began putting together his bent view of reality on this day in 1955.

Graffiti: **How can they say God is dead? We're not even sure about Elvis.**

Joke: A guy goes up to a Salvation Army Santa and asks, "Do you have sinners?"
"Why yes, we do."
"Great," says the guy, throwing ten bucks in the kettle. "Save me a couple for Saturday night!"

DECEMBER

Today's Thought: "I like to buy a four-pack of toilet paper every time I shop, just so I can ask the store clerk this judgment question: 'Would you say I got the right amount of toilet paper for the groceries I just bought?'" -Pat Hazell

Observance/Event: Sports fans rejoice; the instant replay was first introduced on this date in 1963. Sports fans rejoice; the instant replay was first introduced on this date in 1963.

Graffiti: **Santa's helpers are subordinate clauses.**

Joke: Salesman: That's my restaurant bill.
Boss: Well, don't buy any more restaurants.

My ex wrote to me: "Can you delete my number?" I responded: "Who is this?"

DECEMBER

Today's Thought: "A lawyer is a gentleman who rescues your estate from your enemies and keeps it for himself." -Lord Brougham

Observance/Event: Comedian Flip Wilson was born on this day in 1933. His first words were, "What you see is what you get."

Graffiti: With age comes wisdom...like the wisdom to start lying about your age.

Joke: Frack: My mother sent me two sweaters for Christmas and she stopped by while I was wearing one.
Frick: So what's the problem?
Frack: As soon as she saw me, she started in with, "What's the matter? You don't like the other one?"

DECEMBER

Today's Thought: "Health nuts are going to feel stupid someday, lying in hospitals dying of nothing." -Redd Foxx

Observance/Event: St. Louis, Missouri, welcomed Redd Foxx into the world on this date in 1922.

Graffiti: Delete history and start all over again.

Joke: A farmer's dog is missing and the old man is beside himself. His wife advises him to take out an ad in the newspaper, so he does. But a couple of weeks later, there's still no sign of his faithful friend. "What did you put in the ad?" the wife asks.
The farmer answers, "Here boy."

Wouldn't exercise be more fun if calories screamed while you burned them?

DECEMBER

Today's Thought: "Whenever I date a guy, I think, 'Is this the man I want my children to spend their weekends with?'" -Rita Rudner

Observance/Event: It's 15 days until Christmas Day and as you're doing your holiday shopping, remember, it's better to give than to receive. That way you don't have to bother exchanging it.

Graffiti: **Beauty is only sin deep!**

Joke: Knock Knock.
Who's there?
To.
To who?
No, to whom.

DECEMBER

Today's Thought: "Every crowd has a silver lining." -P.T. Barnum

Observance/Event: December is Bingo's Birthday Month, a time to celebrate the invention of Bingo in 1929 by Edwin S. Lowe. Accordingly, we bring you this…"Bingo" is the answer. And the question…"What one word can you say to make a roomful of little old ladies cuss?"

Graffiti: **Help! I'm having an out of money experience.**

Joke: There are three periods in a man's life: he believes in Santa Claus; he doesn't believe in Santa Claus; he is Santa Claus.

Roses are red, violets are blue, God made me pretty, what happened to you?

DECEMBER

Today's Thought: "Democracy means that anyone can grow up to be president and anyone who doesn't grow up can be vice-president." -Johnny Carson

Observance/Event: Hoboken's favorite son and *Doonesbury's* favorite target, Frank Sinatra, was born on this date in 1915. The Chairman of the Board's birthday inspires the graffiti you see below.

Graffiti: **To do is to be- Rousseau.**
To be is to do- Sartre.
Doobedoobedoo- Sinatra.

Joke: Two surgeons were laughing hysterically in a hospital hallway when a dermatologist walked by and asked, "What's so funny?"
One of the surgeons answered, "You wouldn't understand. It's an inside joke."

DECEMBER

Today's Thought: "There's not much good in the worst of us, and so many of the worst of us get the best of us, that the rest of us aren't even worth talking about." -Gracie Allen

Observance/Event: Multi-talented comedic performer Dick Van Dyke entered the world smiling on this date in 1925.

Graffiti: **What's the digital version of "counterclockwise?"**

Joke: Did you hear the one about the family who put up an artificial Christmas tree? When they got up Christmas morning, all the presents under the tree were fake.

When everything's coming your way, you're in the wrong lane and going the wrong way.

DECEMBER

Today's Thought: "I got my hair highlighted because I felt that some strands were more important than others." -Mitch Hedberg

Observance/Event: Patty Duke, who would go on to play identical cousins Patty and Cathy Lane on *The Patty Duke Show,* made her world debut on this day in 1946.

Graffiti: **I drink to forget I drink.**

Joke: Q: Why does Santa use reindeer to pull his sleigh?
A: Because the elephants kept crashing through the roof.

DECEMBER

Today's Thought: "Instead of the John, I call my bathroom the Jim... That way it sounds better when I say I go to the Jim every morning." -Jamie Capria

Observance/Event: That Dorf guy, Tim Conway, was born in 1933.

Graffiti: **Claustrophobia is a fear of Santa Claus.**

Joke: A parrot, a parakeet and a mynah bird go into a bar. They order three beers. The bartender comes back with two beers, one for the parrot and one for the parakeet.
The mynah bird complains, "Hey, where's my beer?"
The bartender says, "Sorry, we don't serve mynahs here."

I can totally keep secrets. It's the people I tell them to that can't.

DECEMBER

Today's Thought: "This guy is so cheap he sends out one Christmas card each year…in the form of a chain letter." -Phyllis Diller

Observance/Event: A reminder: The third Friday of December is Ugly Christmas Sweater Day. Wear it and be proud!

Graffiti: **Let things go to pot. Take a coffee break.**

Joke: A fellow with a dog act goes to Hollywood for an interview with a talent agent. He brings his little Shitzu and St. Bernard into the agent's office. Right away, the Shitzu walks to the middle of the office floor and announces to the agent that he'd like to tell a few jokes. Following one hilarious joke after another, the agent says, "Wow, that Shitzu's unbelievable!"
The dog owner says, "The Shitzu's nothing. The St. Bernard is a ventriloquist!"

DECEMBER

Today's Thought: "I hate the word 'star'. Do you know what 'star' spells backwards?" -Hugh O'Brian

Observance/Event: Today is Wright Brothers Day in honor of the inventors of the airplane. We can thank them for the gift of flight, airline food, lost luggage and interminable delays.

Graffiti: **A fine is a tax for doing wrong. A tax is a fine for doing well.**

Joke: 'Tis the season and some airlines have begun putting mistletoe at the baggage counters. That way you can kiss your luggage goodbye.

I bought a vacuum cleaner six months ago and so far all it's been doing is gathering dust.

DECEMBER

Today's Thought: "Parents were invented to keep children happy by giving them something to ignore." -Ogden Nash

Observance/Event: Movie producer/director Steven Spielberg was born on this date in 1927. In recognition of the occasion, we present this old groaner: How many letters are there in the alphabet? 24...ET went home.

Graffiti: **Whoever invented knock knock jokes deserves a no-bell prize.**

Joke: Husband: Doc, ya gotta help me out. My wife thinks she's a rubber band.
Psychiatrist: Don't worry; she'll soon snap out of it.

DECEMBER

Today's Thought: "I'll tell you what I don't like about Christmas office parties; looking for a new job afterward." -Phyllis Diller

Observance/Event: On this day in 1997, one of the highest grossing movies of all-time opened across theatres in America- *Titanic*. This is not intended to remind you of the sinking feeling that you still have your holiday shopping to do.

Graffiti: **Boat shows have a yacht to offer.**

Joke: There's a new item out there for gift-giving. It's a battery-operated battery. The only problem is the batteries aren't included.

I wasn't originally going to get a brain transplant, but I changed my mind.

DECEMBER

Today's Thought: "If you drink like a fish, don't drive. Swim." -Joe E. Lewis

Observance/Event: Comedic actor Jonah Hill was born on this day in 1983.

Graffiti: **Hummingbirds don't know the words.**

Joke: A guy goes to his friend's costume party with nothing but a naked girl on his back. "What on earth are you supposed to be?" his friend asks.
"I'm a snail."
"What? How can you be a snail when all you've got is that naked girl on your back?"
"That's not any naked girl, pal," his friend says. "That's Michelle."

DECEMBER

Today's Thought: "I came from an Italian house. The refrigerator was always full. I never knew you had to buy food. I thought there were food fairies that came at night." -Ray Romano

Observance/Event: Everybody's been loving Raymond Romano since he was born on this day in 1957.

Graffiti: **Custer was Siouxed.**

Joke: A really big Chia pet walks into a bar, and the bartender says, "What'll it be?"
The Chia pet says, "Anything but water!"

When an employment application asks who is to be notified in case of emergency, I always write, "A very good doctor".

DECEMBER

Today's Thought: "What you don't know would make a great book." -Sydney Smith

Observance/Event: The Beaver's mom, June Cleaver, (aka Barbara Billingsley) was born on this date in 1922.

Graffiti: I've always pictured myself taking selfies.

Joke: It was a frigid winter morning when a woman sent this text to her husband, who had already left for work: "Windows frozen." A little bit later, he sent this reply: "Pour lukewarm water over it." Soon afterwards, she replied: "Computer is completely messed up now."

DECEMBER

Today's Thought: "If I were two-faced, would I be wearing this one?" -Abe Lincoln

Observance/Event: Before the month's out, *The Bathroom Joke Almanac* would like to remind you that this is "Safe Toys and Gifts Month" and to take this opportunity for the following: What was the first thing the rich kid built when he got an erector set for Christmas? A tax shelter.

Graffiti: Running is unnatural...except from predators and to the bathroom.

Joke: "I've finally discovered the magic of Christmas."
"What is it?"
"It's what makes your money disappear."

DECEMBER

Today's Thought: "In suggesting gifts: money is appropriate, and one size fits all." -William Randolph Hearst

Observance/Event: It's Christmas Eve. (And those three words just happen to be the answer to: "What did Adam say to Eve on December 25th?")

Graffiti: **The trouble with the straight and narrow is that there's no place to park.**

Joke: Frick: For Christmas, I bought my son a toy that was guaranteed to be completely unbreakable.
Frack: What happened?
Frick: He used it to break all his other toys!

DECEMBER

Today's Thought: "Santa Claus has the right idea: visit people once a year." -Victor Borge

Observance/Event: It's Christmas Day and you can't hide in the bathroom all day. No matter how long you stay, your relatives will still be there when you come out!

Graffiti: **Beatnik: Santa Claus on Christmas Day.**

Joke: Knock, Knock.
Who's there?
Dexter...
Dexter who?
Dexter halls with boughs of holly...

I'm great at multitasking. I can waste time, be unproductive, and procrastinate all at once.

DECEMBER

Today's Thought: "The trouble with children is that they are not returnable." -Quentin Crisp

Observance/Event: It's National Whiners Day, for those poor souls who whine on line while returning gifts.

Graffiti: **Be sincere even if you have to fake it.**

Joke: Oscar noticed that his buddy Gaylord was depressed. "Cheer up, pal. You may think you have money problems, but I knew a guy who was in the hole for five grand. He wound up driving his vehicle right to the edge of a cliff. A group of very concerned citizens passed a hat around and collected enough to pay off his debt."
"Wow," said Gaylord. "Who were these good Samaritans?"
"The passengers on the bus."

DECEMBER

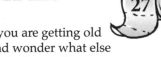

Today's Thought: "You know you are getting old when you stoop to tie your shoes and wonder what else you can do while you're down there." -George Burns

Observance/Event: Hey, boys and girls...It was Howdy Doody time for the first time way back when on this date in 1947. And so the folks who proclaim such things have named this - appropriately enough - Howdy Doody Day.

Graffiti: **Be an organ donor. Give a heart to a lawyer!**

Joke: A man goes to a psychiatrist and tells him that he bites his nails all the time.
The shrink says, "That's not the worst thing in the world."
"But I'm a carpenter."

DECEMBER

Today's Thought: "I've been on a calendar, but I've never been on time." -Marilyn Monroe

Observance/Event: The end of the calendar year is almost upon us, so lest we forget, this is International Calendar Awareness Month. Hence, "Today's thought".

Graffiti: **Thank God I am an atheist!**

Joke: Q: What did the Siamese twins ask for at the golf course?
A: Tee for two

DECEMBER

Today's Thought: "Work is the greatest thing in the world, so we should always save some of it for tomorrow." -Don Herold

Observance/Event: Two of TV's greatest series stars share today as a birthday: Mary Tyler Moore was born in 1937 and Ted Danson drew cheers from his family in 1947. Funny lady Paula Poundstone was also born on this day in 1959.

Graffiti: **Conserve electricity. Thanks a watt!**

Joke: Cop: I'm ticketing you for speeding. You were going at least 90 miles per hour.
Driver: That's ridiculous, officer. I've only been driving for 15 minutes.

DECEMBER

Today's Thought: "My ex and I had a very amicable divorce. I know this because when I wrote the Facebook status 'I'm getting a divorce,' he was the first one to click 'Like.'" -Giulia Rozzi

Observance/Event: Today we celebrate the Festival of Last Minute Enormous Changes. Sounds like you've got a couple of days to get next year's resolutions in order. Or is it a mad rush to fulfill last year's?

Graffiti: **Dieters: A word to the wides is sufficient.**

Joke: Applicant: My father lent me $100,000 for my law education and after my first case, I paid him back every dime.
Personnel Director: That's quite impressive. What case was that?
Applicant: He sued me for it.

DECEMBER

Today's Thought: "An optimist stays up until midnight to see the new year in. A pessimist stays up to make sure the old year leaves." -Bill Vaughan

Observance/Event: It's No Resolution Day. Make up your mind to make no New Year's resolutions. Of course if you do that, you've already made a New Year's resolution. Go figure.

Graffiti: **To all dieters: We wish you a happy new rear!**

Joke: Then there was the guy whose New Year's resolution was to start giving up giving up.

I think they picked me for my motivational skills. Everyone always says they have to work twice as hard when I'm around.